SAPLINGS
and
SPADES

A Woodland Returns

David Parkins

Grosvenor House
Publishing Limited

The right of D. Parkins to be identified as the author of this
work has been asserted in accordance with Section 78
of the Copyright, Designs and Patents Act 1988

The book cover picture is copyright to D. Parkins. Front; Getty Images.
Back; Windy Hill Wood, Northumberland.

This book is published by
Grosvenor House Publishing Ltd
Link House
140 The Broadway, Tolworth, Surrey, KT6 7HT.
www.grosvenorhousepublishing.co.uk

A CIP record for this book
is available from the British Library

ISBN 978-1-78623-172-7

To Elizabeth

Author's Notes

I have written in good faith and naturally assume readers dress appropriately for woodland activities, use personal protection equipment and follow woodland bio-security procedures when necessary.

When subjects relate directly to the Wood they are written as Wood or Woodland. Otherwise, they are treated as common nouns.

The trees are referred to by their popular names.

Superscript numbers, e.g.[1] are references to notes in Chapter Fifteen.

Weights and measures are imperial with approximate metric equivalents.

References conclude the book, the Wood species list being the final entry.

Contents

Illustrations

Introduction

I was often asked why I planted a wood. It was not a straightforward question and invited simplistic answers. My inquisitors were not satisfied with global warming platitudes and pursued their interrogations. How do you plant a new wood on a grass field and what made you do it in the first place? These people were serious and their interest genuine; I started to think.

I have always been fascinated by woods. I played in them as a boy, was deployed to them in the army and maintained them for charity. Other events, a saddening memory, injury and cheerful companionship played their role. Somehow all merged and in an offbeat moment I decided, illogically, to plant a wood. I began my research.

I soon realised there was more to woodland creation than planting saplings. With deceptive ease I became the owner, designer, manager and factotum of the project. I was the man behind the spade with a story to tell.

My tale starts in the early sixties and finishes over fifty years later in the young Wood. I detail the influential events leading to my decision, the hunt for a site and what I discovered there. I recall my thoughts about the wood I wanted, how I planted it, the disasters that followed and the structures I built. In between lie observations and anecdotes, whilst useful practical details have their own chapter away from the main text.

So here I am writing to those wanting, or wondering what it is like, to plant a new wood of their own from absolutely nothing. As with every narrative, events may not necessarily be in strict sequence and this leads me to another woodland topic; I excavated three ponds.

Welcome to the Wood,
David Parkins.
Northumberland.

1

A Whimsical Notion

As a young boy, I lived in Kent. My friends and I played in the local woods that camouflaged an abandoned army depot. These woods were special; the depot's concrete tracks were intact, and we raced our bikes recklessly along them.

One day it was different: as we bicycled to the wood, diesel exhaust fumes wafted across the lane and we heard the heavy growl of large engines. We arrived at the gate; the trees were gone, and our way was blocked by an embankment of fresh earth. Scrambling up to the top, we were halted by advancing bulldozers. We stood stunned as their massive curved blades tore up our tracks and smashed our trees aside, leaving a desolate wake destined to be the Sevenoaks bypass. Nothing was spared; the trees were flung into mangled heaps, doused with oil and set alight. We were engulfed by dense black clouds of acrid smoke, and blaming it for our tears, we went unhappily to play in a different wood.

Our woe over the tracks soon vanished; a stream ran through this wood. Building dams, with the associated ponds and bridges, were added to tree climbing, dens, conker fights and swings. These were carefree moments, we were allowed to be boys and the woods encouraged it. Less laid-back and somewhat sterner when it came to motivation was school.

Our schoolmistress was an enthusiastic teacher whose classroom displayed a large map of the world's forests pinned on the wall. She talked about the trees' individual characteristics and the international timber trade. She explained the modern importance of wood, its historical use in ships and took the class to see the *Cutty Sark*.

In the early sixties the *Cutty Sark* was preserved, unlike today, as a proper sailing ship. I will never forget the masts stretching heavenwards, the wooden deck underfoot, the full-size ship's wheel and the oak barrel full of hard tack biscuits. I imagined I was the intrepid captain ordering full sail ahead. What young boy wouldn't?

Life moved on, and before the bypass was finished, my father's work brought us all to Newcastle-upon-Tyne. The family settled into the bustling city; my brother, sister and I into our new schools. We were soon exploring Northumberland.

Northumberland is a magnificent, windswept county of haunting beauty and turbulent history. Wide, boundless skies, wild vistas of hills, moorland and forest captivate the senses. Steep-sided valleys shelter ancient woodlands, their rivers flowing to a coastline of golden beaches, fishing villages, castles and islands. I adopted the county as home.

At school, trees were a serious subject, earning valuable marks in exams. I learnt of photosynthesis, likening it to making wood out of thin air. Equally as remarkable was the trees' ability to transpire, lifting water out of the ground, expelling it from the stomata underneath their leaves all silently without a pump. Physics added more on timber's material properties. Our maths master set us his 'ligneous problems' on timber processing with saw waste percentages, and transport costs thrown in for extra measure. I was taught woodwork; the lessons learnt on accurate marking out and sharp tools remain with me today.

I liked trees. However, my main interest lay with machinery and I wanted to be a mechanic. The army offered the qualifications I sought, and I enlisted into the Royal Electrical and Mechanical Engineers.

Plate 1: February manoeuvres, Germany, 1975.

2

I trained as a tank fitter and was posted to Germany. Apart from hiding stores, the military regarded woods as appropriate places to repair tanks. There were many forests on the German plain and my unit was deployed regularly to them. I was back in the woods, working outside in all weathers.

Tanks were demanding machines to repair, and, hidden deep in the forest without full workshop facilities, the task was more exacting. There was an ominous mood within these woods; they were no longer a playground, but a backdrop to the rehearsal of war. We took our duties seriously and the trees, indifferent as ever, could not have cared less.

I enjoyed my work but recognised life was greater than mending tanks. I completed my service and returned to Northumberland. I desired to move on and joined the police.

Busy years followed, and my woodland memories slumbered half-forgotten. I married Elizabeth and remain happily so. We bought a house, planted the garden and maintained an allotment; I passed professional exams and worked shifts. Late one rainy night my circumstances began to change.

I attended a call and saw a thief fleeing down a back street. I chased and caught him, slipping on the wet cobbles as I did so. We crashed down and my knees twisted apart as he landed on me. My colleagues arrived quickly taking the thief to jail and me, in shocked pain, to hospital. I was not ungrateful for the arrest; the injuries were my unfortunate bad luck.

The knees healed, and I resumed work. As years passed the joints grew increasingly uncomfortable. The injury weakened the cartilages, putting pressure on the kneecaps. If not agonising enough, my knees collapsed intermittently, once sending me headlong—and fortunately, unhurt—down a flight of stairs. The police surgeon referred me to a consultant.

The consultant confirmed the injuries as chronic retro-patella pain and offered an operation. I declined as it risked leaving me in a wheelchair for life. Surgery or not, I was declared unfit for police service and pensioned off.

I assessed the situation. I retired over a decade earlier than expected and I did not want to give up and get fat. The first priority was getting my legs back into some sort of shape; the physiotherapist was supportive and gave me a set of exercises designed to keep my injuries manageable.

I slogged away at the exercises, re-discovered the joys of walking and brushed up on my woodworking skills building a workshop in the garden. I polished my MGC sports car and fixed old valve radios. Nonetheless, I missed the sense of contribution I had felt in the army and the police. I wanted a purpose; the more outdoors the challenge, the better. A local television announcement led the way.

Wallington Hall, a regional National Trust property, was advertising for volunteer gardeners. I knew the property from family explorations and it was a favourite. Set in countryside, surrounded by woodlands, the Hall wanted help. I offered my services and was engaged.

The dedicated staff were affable and understood my necessity to operate at a steady pace. I was coping with my knees and relished the purposeful physical activity.

Besides looking after the grounds, the gardeners were responsible for the woodlands around the house. I was in the woods again, pruning branches and burning brash. I qualified as a chainsaw operator and assisted the chainsaw gang with thinning and felling. There was ample work for me to do.

During one lunch break, our chat turned to forestry. I joked that no wood was complete without tanks and they did not usually knock trees down. I described the obliteration I witnessed as a boy and our discussion changed to the way modern roads were built. None of us were anti-road and were pleased the days of razing a path for them were over. Nowadays there was sympathy towards the landscape and care taken to replenish the trees lost under the tarmac...Then it struck me:

"I can replace those!" I exulted to myself.

Reaction immediately dismissed the sentiment. Replacing a fraction of the woodlands flattened over thirty years before - with, how and for what? No land, little experience and a pair of wrecked knees; pull yourself together man! I did, and the Spirit soared.

"Let's do it!" Spirit rejoiced, "Let's just do it!"

The jubilant cry echoed around the inside of my head. I found my goal.

I was going to buy a field and plant a wood.

2

Reconnaissance

I gazed at the bleak moorland, my back to the gale force wind. No trees or sheep in sight, even the drystone walls looked miserable. The rain started as I trudged back to the van and became torrential as I climbed in; the windscreen opaque with the downpour. I looked at the agent's blurb and sighed: the trees would demand guy ropes to survive here.

I reflected it might be best to visit sites in foul weather. Before my field enquiries began, I had made a list of what I thought a suitable site should be. The moorland scored highly on size, access and price. There were new fences, undulating ground, reasonable soil and clear mobile phone reception. I was prepared to waive the twenty-mile limit from home for a promising site; this one, even by Northumbrian weather standards, was far too exposed.

I dove off down the valley, passing land where I had been outbid. The sales leaflet proclaimed 'as a whole or in lots' and I bid low for a field. My audacity went unrewarded, the agent accepting an offer for the entire one-hundred-and-twenty-acre site. The out-bidder, who later became a friend, was also planting a wood, simply on a grander scale.

My scale was six to twelve acres. I was dealing at the bottom end of the market, where the prices were low for a reason. I was wary of covenants and local authority searches. It reinforced my desire to have a solicitor scrutinise any title deeds I was interested in. Besides the paperwork, there may be practical objections.

Flooding, mine shafts, pipelines and pylons were real perils. Perhaps the site was near a main road, crisscrossed by public foot paths or purely flat, dull, polluted, surrounded by buildings and used as a tip.

I would hire a surveyor if necessary to check acreage, inspect buildings and disused quarry faces etc. In the beginning, I did not know what I may find and, in the end, did not use those services.

In 2002, Google Earth was in its infancy and I relied on Ordnance Survey maps. I knew maps, like Google Earth today, were understandably not up to date. Two maxims sprang to mind: *'time spent on reconnaissance is seldom wasted'* and *'caveat emptor! – let the buyer beware!'* In other words, go and have a look and never be afraid to walk away saying no thank you.

The 1:25000 scale, or 2.5 inches to the mile, maps were readily available. These gave details of contours, landscape features and field boundaries. The 1:2500 scale maps, used by the Land Registry for title deeds, gave individual field areas. I used the modern editions to locate the site and gain an idea of how it laid on the landscape. Older editions were examined for historical detail.

I found the 19th Century OS editions in the Northumberland County Archives. The 1866 and 1897 editions, at twenty-five inches to the mile, illustrate the ground superbly. The 1866 version marks individual trees on field boundaries, reminiscent of the days when artillery used trees as target markers.

I was in no hurry and did not set a deadline. I expected a long haul and prepared for setbacks. I studied the land for sale adverts in regional papers, farmer's magazines and visited rural estate agents.

The newspaper ads revealed two probable sites; one was an infilled quarry, the other adjacent to a railway station. The quarry site was landscaped sympathetically, following the natural contours. I was enthusiastic until enquiries revealed all the new trees were stolen from the location.

As I drove to the railway station site, I imagined commuting to my wood by train. I was disabused of the idea, and owning the site, by the in situ burnt out cars. Thereafter, I underlined 'security' on my check list.

It was the estate agents who provided most information when I explained my intent to plant a wood and asked about slow selling land. The bottom drawers of filing cabinets were opened enthusiastically and I was handed ageing sales brochures. One dossier stood out and I went to see.

The three-acre riverside field included fishing rights, a ruined mill, and a stand of Scots pine all enclosed by an undamaged drystone wall. Entry was by foot, vehicle access negotiable and all for the price of a cheap second-hand car. Even so, the money was incredibly low.

The site, by covenant, was a garden to a house a hundred yards distant. A covenant, or legal contract, has two parties. The first is the beneficiary and the other carries the burden. Here the burden fell on the field owner, who did not have full control of the land. I asked a solicitor if covenants could be removed.

The answer was a complex yes. In order to remove a covenant, or be released from it, every beneficiary must be contacted. These were the house owners and a company who controlled the mineral rights to the site. Other beneficiaries may be more elusive, taking diligent enquiries and national press notices to track down.

After all the beneficiaries were identified, it was best to negotiate the release, usually a cash settlement with their legal costs on top of mine. Should agreement fail, the whole case could be taken to the Lands Tribunal, an expensive procedure. The second-hand car was becoming a Ferrari, the price of forests. I said no thanks and walked away a wiser man.

I sold the MGC to help fund my Woodland venture. I bought the car as a wreck and enjoyed renovating it. The classic car market was buoyant, and I soon handed the keys to the new owner. Other funds were good providence; a bargain job lot of vintage radios included several rare and desirable models.

I continued the site hunt. I scrutinised and rejected five plots; three were crossed by electricity poles, the fourth was in the middle of an industrial estate and the fifth came with planning permission for a market garden.

I located the market garden land by accident. A 'For Sale' sign in a hedgerow pointed to a worthy looking field. The planning permission put the cost beyond my budget. I passed the details on to friends, who bought the field and founded their own successful plant nursery.

Next up was a pleasant site, having road access, a stream and surrounding woodland.

I approached the agent and was told the site was off the market. Trusting to luck, I asked if there was anything similar for sale. She reached into the in-tray and handed me the brochure for Gorfenletch Farm.

Plate 2: Gorfenletch Farm Road Sign.

3

Field Number Three

The brochure was encouraging. Gorfenletch Farm was located off the A1 and under twenty miles from home. Most of the journey was dual carriageway, a change from the other sites.

The farm was for sale in lots after an auction failed to sell it as a whole. A six-and-a-half-acre field, half a mile in from the road, attracted my interest. A private stone track led from the road, past the farm buildings to the field gate. A covenant guaranteed access.

I related my experience of covenants to the agent. She assured me there was no nonsense regarding gardens and the freehold title was absolute. I thanked her, and with the sales literature as proof of permission to look, made my way to the farm.

I appreciated the straightforward journey. On the day, it was one more reconnaissance, the twelfth I thought, as I turned off the road and drove towards the farm buildings.

I parked up near two houses and a cottage. After curving slightly, the track ran straight to the field, the stone surface overgrown with grass. I thought it best to check the track by foot and walked to the field. The fields, including the one I was interested in, were full of weighty, round hay bales awaiting collection. If the track to the potential Wood was fit for large tractors and hay trailers, it should be fine for future timber extraction.

Fifty metres from the site gate, a white post in the hedgerow marked the underground route of a high-pressure gas pipeline, unmentioned in the sales information.

I knew tree planting was prohibited ten metres either side of a pipeline and I never desired a twenty-metre-wide treeless wayleave running through my wood. I turned to face the far hedgerow and saw a second marker. The pipeline ran at a diverging angle from the field and fifty metres was the closest it came. No pylons or wires crossed overhead, and, comforted by these facts, I opened the gate.

The stone track gave way to grass and continued west alongside the bottom hedgerow. It was a private right of way across the farm and would not interfere with the Wood. The track left the field, ran parallel to a backfilled ditch to a wicket gate on the farm boundary where it stopped. The narrow gate was for horse and foot use only.

The nearest lane was two hundred yards away behind a hedgerow. The stone track, straddled by three gates and running past inhabited houses, was the only vehicle access in and out of the field, an advantage when it came to securing the site.

The field for sale was under grass. The soil was firm underfoot with shallow puddles left here and there by recent rain. The top soil was compacted and would require breaking up or being ripped to help surface drainage; I would hire a contractor for the work before tree planting began. The surface would remain irregular until the winter frosts and the ripping plough would expose stones for removal.

The ground rose gently northwards; around mid-field it dipped to lose sight of the entrance and flattened out approaching the north fence. Beyond the fence the ground remained level for about forty yards before rising, as coarse pasture, to moorland.

The post, wire and sheep net fences were in reasonable condition. The north, south and west hedgerows were reduced to a few hawthorn trees on grass banks. The north bank was home to yarrow, or wound-wart, a small leaved herb with astringent properties. The east hedgerow contained most of the vegetation including two large ash trees.

One ash was a healthy strong tree with masses of keys on its branches. The second ash, eighty yards north along the hedgerow, was a bulbous, hollow veteran, its ancient limbs entwined with the new and 'beef-steak' fungus infested the trunk. The tree was marked on the 1866 OS map; even then it was noteworthy enough for the cartographers. I spotted a weasel fleeing into a burrow under the roots. I continued my survey finding crab apple trees and blackthorn bushes. The best find lay ahead.

The hawthorn tree displayed rounded three-lobed leaves, different than the normal tooth-shaped ones. I sent a cutting to the Forestry Commission's research station at Alice Holt Forest, Hampshire. They identified it as midland hawthorn, a scarcity in Northumberland. I speculated how it arrived there.

The midland bush was in line with the other gnarled hawthorns. It was likely to have been planted with them when the land was enclosed at the beginning of the nineteenth century. However it came, it made me realise the importance of recording the tree species I planted in the new Wood. References

An attractive feature was a piped water supply to a trough. Tool cleaning crossed my mind and I left the field, closing the gate behind me. It fell off its hinges, as if to alert me there was other work to be done before I washed any spades.

I liked the site and returned the following day with a spade and a pH soil acidity meter.

One of the Forestry Commission's guidelines for tree planting states: 'any reasonable soil will do'. I walked across the field with the spade and, lifting various sods, measured the pH. All revealed earth worms and a mid-range pH reading of seven. This would definitely 'do' for the trees.

I saw the neighbours, who were friendly and wished me well. They informed me the track was muddy in winter, which was something I could live with.

A surveyor advised me the asking price was fair. I telephoned the agent to make my offer. He enquired what I wanted the field for. I said planting a wood, and he asked me the colour of my money. I replied cash, preferably by cheque. He cheered up and accepted. We exchanged details and, subject to contract, the field was mine.

I put the phone down. The search was over, and if all went well, I could start planning my Wood. I trusted I would not be gazumped or the searches reveal horrors. I pondered over continuing my search.

I inspected eleven locations before Gorfenletch, would the thirteenth have been better? Risks are risks. I placed the maps aside and dismissed sites from my thoughts.

The solicitor's report confirmed absolute freehold title and guaranteed access. Two covenants obliged me to share the costs of track maintenance and water supply. The field was open countryside and the local authority search revealed an agreeable list of 'no's' such as:

Archaeological ruins, conservation areas, landfill locations, mineshafts, National Parks, opencast operations, public rights of way and sites of special scientific interest.

I signed the formal documents and handed over the cheque for the 6.57-acre (2.66ha) field. I now owned field no.3 of the old Gorfenletch Farm, the gorse, s was once f, by the slow stream, letch.

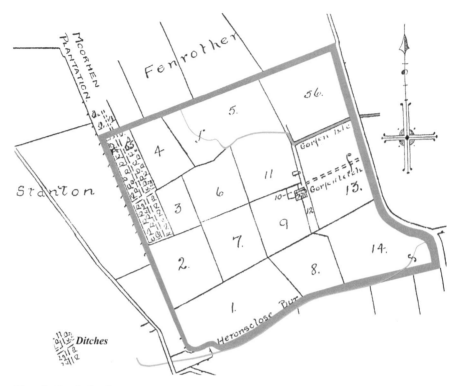

Plate 3: Gorfenletch Farm Conveyance map, 1919.

It was not the final land I bought for the Wood. Over a decade and in two increments, the Woodland area increased by three acres (1.2ha). Whatever the future, I was free to plan the Wood and explore the locality.

I had a hunch that the fields and ditches had stories to tell…

4

Of Fields...

The rusty horseshoe was all to show for an August's afternoon work. I switched off the metal detector; my search for gold under the field was in vain. The morning had been more fruitful. I had followed the course of the Gorfen Letch, reconnoitred the nearest wood and discovered an abandoned airfield.

The Gorfen Letch is an open stream draining east across the farm towards a culvert under the main road. Shortly after, the stream joins the River Lyne on its way to the North Sea. Within the farm, the Letch is joined by two tributaries draining the higher land to the north. These looked dry and I went to explore.

I started my expedition at the culvert. It was a damp, overgrown spot at the bottom of the road embankment. The stream was funnelled into the culvert by concrete banks, making the confined water run faster down the narrow pipe. Despite the stream's low level, I doubted if wildlife could use the channel as a corridor. Nature was overlooked when the road was straightened in the sixties, the Sevenoaks bypass era.

The stream formed a natural division between the fields and was fenced on the south bank. The bankside trees were hawthorn, ash and alder; there was no gorse. I was beginning to mull over the name when I met the tributaries.

Both were shallow north-westward rising valleys. The stream beds were infilled, and, two feet beneath the grass surface, six-inch clay pipes drained into the stream. I continued upstream, and, about a hundred yards away from the Wood field, the stream came out of another pipe.

The map showed the open stream stopping here. Despite the dry

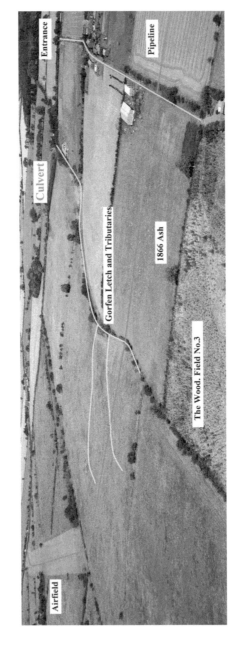

Plate 4: I started my expedition at the culvert. ©air images ltd.

weather, the flat belt of lush grass was soft underfoot. I followed it past the future wood's north fence to the westernmost boundary of the farm where I could see a gorse thicket.

The thicket straddled the fence lengthways for over forty yards and my faith in the place name was restored. I suspected a lot of gorse was cleared when the land was drained and sustained grazing kept it down since. The following spring the gorse thicket was home to a pair of oystercatchers, who have returned each year since.

I turned north, walking up the three-hundred-yard grass slope towards Moorhen Plantation, depicted as a mixed deciduous woodland on the modern OS map. The 1897 OS edition showed the plantation as coniferous and extending down the slope past the west side of the Wood. I was on deforested ground. The 1866 map showed no trees on the site; the pines had been and gone. Moorhen Plantation was not the only one named after birds.

Within a square mile, lay the Coote, Cuckoo, Snipe (formally a tile factory, the clay pits now ponds) and Woodcock Plantations. There was a Tank Plantation (water storage type) and a wood called Scrog (stunted bush). Further afield was Hangingleaves Wood and an oval shaped plantation named Egg.

Plantation is the general term for a wood planted by man, and judging by the maps, I was in plantation territory. I suspected the local soil was poor, and while there some arable fields in the vicinity, the farms were chiefly grass. Cattle, sheep, horses and hay governed here; the woods providing shelter belts and game.

I continued the gentle ascent. The farm boundary fence separated the trees from the pasture, it was an abrupt transition from field to woodland. I entered the dim wood.

The regularly spaced birch trees sported fungus on their trunks. A few dead larch and scrubby hawthorn were scattered about. Sheep were munching the grass floor and I saw no saplings. There was a forlorn atmosphere about the place, the neglected gamebird feeders adding to the melancholy.

Several years after this initial gloomy visit, I revisited the plantation and saw new honeysuckles and field roses growing on the eastern boundary, which had not been there on my first visit. Earlier, I planted the same two species in my Wood and they had already given several

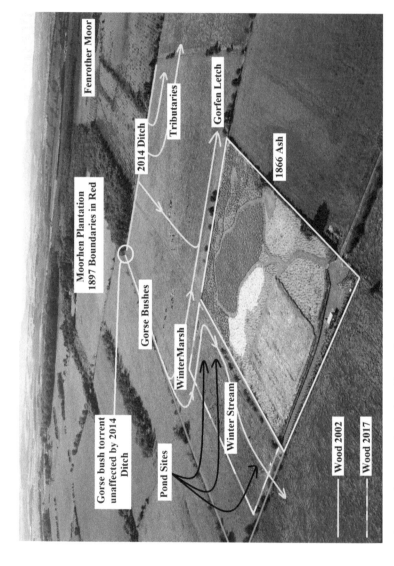

Plate 5: *The water divided itself into four torrents.* ©*air images ltd*

16

seasons of fruit. I claim their natural distribution as a Woodland success.

I returned to the tree line and turned east headed towards the second pipeline marker I had spotted on my first visit. I reached the white post and stood at the end of an abandoned runway.

I was looking at a First World War airfield used by 36 Squadron Royal Flying Corps. The airfield was one of several used for coastal defence by the Squadron, noted for shooting down a Zeppelin in 1917. The pipeline continued underneath the runway, and I went to lunch, promising myself to return in winter to see the drainage in action.

It was a sunny December day. The heavy rain cleared at dawn and I returned to my August vantage point by the plantation. I no longer stood on a dry meadow; my wellies were ankle deep in surface flood water flowing off Fenrother Moor and south to the Woodland.

The water divided itself into four torrents. Two fed the tributaries of the Gorfen Letch. The third and fourth swamped the flat stretch of land north of the unflooded Wood. The surface water extended west towards the gorse thicket, explaining the oystercatchers' interest and attracting mine.

There was a small rise in the land between the Wood and the gorse thicket boundary. The rise made a natural dam forming a swampy reservoir, or winter marsh, feeding the Gorfen Letch draining east and a winter stream flowing south adjacent to the west boundary of the Wood. The stream filled three shallow depressions in the ground and I noted these as potential pond sites.

I followed the stream down past the Wood, across the track and onto the adjacent field. I spotted a flooded hollow west off Gorfenletch land and went over to see.

A foot of water covered the grass. I prodded the submerged pasture with my stick and it slid quickly into the sodden ground. This was no place to walk. The grass proved the ground was dry in summer and no winter streams were running to or from the hollow. I dismissed it as a seasonal quagmire and if my stick was anything to go by, one to avoid. I turned about and, retracing my footsteps back to the field, forgot it. The quag did not forget me.

The 1897 OS map as well as the 1919 conveyance plan showed Moorhen Plantation intersected with ditches. Only traces of them remained by the bottom track and on the western boundary of the farm. I assumed they were replaced by a new drainage system when the Gorfenletch part of the plantation was converted into pasture. I speculated when the deforestation happened.

The 1924 and 1942 OS maps show most of the pines standing, whilst the 1954 edition records them clear felled and the deciduous part of the planation in place. It is believed the pines were cleared for pitprops by Italian POWs during the Second World War. Their camp, four miles north of the Wood, is now a holiday caravan park.

The field was unaffected by the flood waters and I continued planting trees. The seasons passed and I received many visitors for whom I wrote Woodland pamphlets. These were popular, provoking questions from the guests and my appearance on morning TV. The idea of this book was beginning to form, and I returned to the Northumberland County Archives to see what more the records held for Gorfenletch.

... and Ditches

Northumberland County Archives, N.C.A, are housed within the Woodhorn Colliery Museum, ten miles east of the Wood. The pit wheels remain standing above the closed shaft and I remembered the fate of the Gorfenletch pines. Bad weather days are best to visit archives, and the day was no exception. A bitter February north wind swirled around the pit head and pockets of last night's frost lingered in the shadows. I made my way to the air-conditioned comfort of the custom-built archive and was welcomed by the helpful staff.

The reference book section included a copy of the 1887 History and Directory of Northumberland which describes Gorfenletch as:

...a hamlet, one farm and one cottage. Sandy loam with clay subsoil, varies in quality, laid down to grass. R.V (rateable value) £800."

The farmhouse and cottage stand whilst the steading has been converted into a house. The entry confirmed my suspicion of poor soil.

The varying quality of the soil was due to the mixed glacial deposits of clay sand and stones forming the subsoil: 'diamicton' in geological terms. The grass pasture was not without merit; Gorfenletch Farm was renowned for high quality sheep.

Sheep graze the surrounding fields. They get used to seeing me in the Wood and, if I am working near the boundaries, follow me from the other side of the fence. There was some pond maintenance to do. The sheep were on top of the hill with a clear view of me in waders walking into the pond. The flock stampeded to the fence and, standing in a half circle, bleated at me until I waded out of the water. Assured, they trotted back up the hill. I was not their shepherd but was, nevertheless, touched by their concern.

In 1887 the farm was part of Lord Portland's Northumberland estate. The archivist suggested I looked up the estate records for additional information. Amongst the papers I found a letter filed as 'ditch at bottom of Moorhen Plantation'. I opened the envelope and read the letter, dated June 1908, from Mr Wilson, the wealthy merchant owner of the neighbouring Stanton Estate, to Mr Sample, Lord Portland's land agent.

Mr Wilson was complaining on behalf of his tenant, Mr Rutherford. Mr Wilson stated a drain near the wicket gate in the Duke's wood *(Moorhen Plantation)* was blocked and flooding his tenants' land. The flooding formed *a sort of bog* which Mr Rutherford claimed was killing his ewes. *See* references: Wilson's Letter of Complaint.

My memory flashed; the quag returned to haunt me as an antique letter read in a cosy archive; I could do nothing other than investigate. I returned to the deforested Duke's wood and made my way to the wicket gate and started my search.

I felt certain the backfilled ditch running parallel to the track was the *'drain near the wicket gate'* (replaced in 2012) referred to by Mr Wilson. I surmised the other ditches may not have helped either.

There was no surface water leaving Gorfenletch under the gate. I walked across the wet field to a manhole cover and lifted the lid. Water was flowing in and out of an inspection chamber via underground pipes. One pipe came from the direction of the gate and left the chamber under a cattle track. The damp track curved southwards around a natural rise and into *the bog at the bottom*.

I recalled the torrent pouring off the moor and my stick sliding into the swamp. I visualised the ditch water surging relentlessly under the gate, creating the deadly ooze of the mutton murdering marsh. I checked the ground for fatalities and, seeing none, left the scene. This was once Mr Wilson's land, Mr Rutherford's sheep, the Duke's estate and a forest to pasture clearance. I wondered who'd paid for the drains.

The winter was followed by a wet spring. The marsh remained flooded until the aerial survey of the Wood in July. Within a week the bog at the bottom was dry and has not re-appeared since.

In 1919 the Duke sold the 242-acre (98ha) farm for £3,200 to the estate who sold the Woodland site to me. Whether sheep, soil, ditches, or drains engrossed his Lordship as he signed the conveyance might never be known.

Whatever befell the plantation ditches, Gorfenletch was not rid of them. In the mid-seventies a new ditch spanned the breadth of the farm

Plate 6: The Bog at the Bottom, July 2012. ©air images ltd.

21

to bury a natural gas pipeline. The soil was shallow, and the engineers blasted through bedrock to achieve the two-metre depth for the trench.

The explosions destroyed the farm's spring water supply. A replacement borehole was sunk to supply the farm with water. New pipes connected the borehole to troughs, including the one in the future Wood. The fields were restored and the white posts in the hedgerows marked the pipeline's route.

In 2014 a second ditch was dug along the southern edge of Moorhen Plantation running eastwards towards the pipeline. *See* Plate 5. A new tenant was re-instating one of the 19th century ditches to control the winter surface water flowing off Fenrother Moor.

The contractor arrived on site and the pipeline engineers became aware of the work. As the ditch came closer to the marker, officials appeared demanding a written explanation.

Water, ditches, letters; Gorfenletch had seen them before and lost its trees. I was replacing those and reminded myself of what I was going to do.

6

Thinking about Woods

I signed the delivery note for the second shipping container. The first container, a 1971 conversion to a works cabin, complete with gas fire, lights and stove, had arrived the day before. The second was a plain container fitted with a secure padlocking system, ideal for tools and equipment.

The tools soon accumulated in their container; I started with a tree planting spade and ended up with a wood chipper. In between came the rest and a ride-on brush cutter.

The containers were an excellent start to the first winter planting season, giving me a ready-made warm shelter, secure storage and an operational Woodland base. Over the years I re-fitted both containers, the renovations incorporating a log shed, stoves and hardstanding. [1-3]
See Plate 9

I was eager to start planting and paused to think of my objectives. It was an excuse to test the stove for a brew and the new tap I fitted on to the trough stand pipe.

The water was pumped at mains pressure from the borehole near the farm buildings four hundred yards away. I filled the kettle and, keen to extend the water pipe to the cabin, counted my paces back to the containers. I wrote a few plumbing notes and, with a mug of tea in hand, concentrated on my main thoughts of the day.

I was in no hurry to establish the Wood and if this took longer than others, so be it. I considered asking friends for help. By law any person who works for you, paid or not, is your employee and I could not afford the obligatory liability insurance. If I was to run a solo project, it would not be a reclusive one.

Plate 7: Tools, Tree Planting and Maintenance.

From top left: wheelbarrow, sapling protection pipe, grubbing mattock, tree spade with fibre glass handle, stake driver, knapsack sprayer, bow saw, loppers, pruning saw without scabbard, gloves, warm hat, staple gun with staples, pruning knife, secateurs, club hammer.

Left inset: logging tongs, the four-pivot gripping action makes it easier to handle heavy sleepers and logs.

Right inset: weed-wiper, the hollow handle is filled with herbicide solution which feeds the t-shaped wick as it is wiped across the weeds.

I invited family, friends, schools and woodland societies. Their company was welcomed, as were their dogs.

Two guests arrived and helped their elderly dog out of the car. After a snuffle she was off running amongst the trees. A loud splash told us she had found a pond. We caught up to see her shake herself dry before scampering back to Mum and Dad, wagging tail up high. She jumped back into the car and fell asleep, dreaming of the rabbits she did not quite catch.

Remembering my boyhood, I wanted to arrange school visits and many took place over the following years. Judging by the children's thank you letters, the visits were a hit. Their latest trips, with the trees taller and the ponds excavated, fell into a routine:-

Plate 8: Machinery.
Top Left: Grass control, ride-on brush cutter and strimmer. Right: Power barrow for general purpose work.
Centre: Wood chipper with two hours worth of chips.
Bottom: Chain saw, hedge cutter and 16 ft (4.9m) pole saw.

Come the day, a crowd of boisterous children arrived at the gate. It was time to let off steam, and races around the tracks were organised by their teachers. Between the races I explained what the different tree species were and what they were used for. The cricket bat willows and the cherries were favourites. Maybe the CBWs were tall like the *Cutty Sark's* masts and the red cherries looked far more delicious than hard tack.

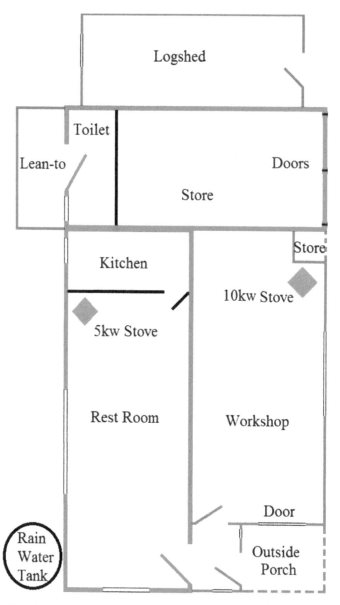

Plate 9: The shed floor plan, original containers in red. I replaced the rest room container's double doors with a wooden side wall. Rain water is collected for diluting herbicide. The log shed has a transparent roof and an automatic opening window to utilise the greenhouse effect for fire wood drying.

The children were interested in the ponds, asking were there any fish, how they were excavated, and did I get wet digging them? One said it was very thoughtful to help frogs with ponds and was I paid for it! My answer was a kindly no, I did not have any grants.

In 2002, woodland establishment [4] grants were available from the Forestry Commission. The application process was a points system and the field failed to qualify. I would buy the saplings, stakes and shelters and be free of the obligations attached to public money.

I was unlikely to make much cash out of a six-acre wood, and a commercial aspect was advantageous. The Wood was capable of growing valuable saw logs and I would manage the trees accordingly. Saw logs take years to mature and for the shorter term I would grow coppice [5]. Woods with financial worth were more liable to survive than not. It was an achievable aim and necessary with the advent of climate change.

My concern with climate change was the ability of trees to acclimatise - some may do better than others. A mixed species woodland in good condition was the best bet and compatible with other aspects of woodland design.

New woodlands tend to be planted all at once and age equally. I re-collected the poor regenerative state of the even aged Moorhen Plantation and wanted to prevent the Wood following a similar fate. Keeping the sheep out was easy. I needed a rolling plan to replace trees, or a Continuous Cover Forestry, CCF, strategy.

Within forests and woodlands managed under CCF, individual or small groups of trees are felled. The canopy is opened up for re-generation, either by restocking or self-seeding, and the result is a healthy, mixed aged woodland with a generous understorey.

I could mitigate the even age syndrome a little. It would be impossible for me to plant six acres with over seven thousand trees in one winter. I divided the Woodland into stands and tracks. Each stand would have a dominant species with others for diversity. I would plant twelve hundred trees per acre per year. This meant a six-year span between the oldest and youngest trees with a six-foot spacing between each tree.

In the occasion, I planted over twice the number of trees. I spent an extra eight years replacing sapling casualties from assorted causes and stocking the three-acre expansion. I ended with a fourteen-year span between the first and last plantings. The six-foot spacing fosters straighter growth, though if left alone, the trees would grow into a dark, unattractive wood.

A sustainable wood must please the eye. After canopy cover, I'd thin the trees to develop the light, airy woodland necessary for CCF. Wildlife would benefit, timber extraction problems ease and capital value increase. Widely spaced woods are less liable to wind throw; the Great Storm of 1987 annihilated densely packed woodlands in Kent and I did not want mine to follow suit.

The Woodland was four hundred feet above sea level and exposed to gales. It would take a while for the boundary trees to develop into effective shelter belts. I could expect some wind damage. It was an ongoing matter - the posts and ties could wait. I used these several times to support apple trees and questioned if my gardening skills were sufficient for the assignment. As it happened, it was a matter of magnitude and my expertise evolved to match the circumstances.

Founding a new wood is an industrial operation. Clothes, tools and machines must be high quality, or they will dangerously disintegrate. Bonfires are hot and massive. Weeds not massacred by herbicide are uprooted and left to rot where they fall. Saplings are planted by the hundred and, unlike young garden trees, depend on summer rainfall. I'd sooner think of wildlife than droughts.

I was eager to encourage wildlife. A priority was to restore the hedgerows and I planned a wildflower meadow. Ponds were initially out of the question; it was three years before the winter stream site came up for sale. I wanted the wild creatures to take the Wood as their stronghold and sally forth into the countryside with attitude; a noble belief if ever there was. I returned to earth and considered the type and classification of my Wood.

My deliberations were disrupted by the screaming roar of an RAF Tornado flying fast two hundred feet above the track, missiles and bombs clearly visible on the underside of its wings. It was not unusual to see jets passing overhead on their way to the training ranges and today was my turn for the low pass. I waved to the fighter and in the corner of my eye was there a biplane taking off from the deserted airfield, the goggled pilot returning my wave?

The type of woodland is a description of the wood as a whole or a brief review of the trees and soil. I thought an 'oak, cherry, hazel diamicton woodland' was a mouthful and chose the overall portrayal of 'standards with coppice'.

Woodland classification is diverse; the Royal Forestry Society's excellent Glossary of Tree Terms, takes a page to list the UK categories. Here is a brief summary:

First up are the primary woodlands. These are the rare remains of the post-glacial wildwood. It is likely they were harvested regularly and left alone to regenerate.

Following are the ancient woodlands which were in existence before 1600AD. If you own a wood mentioned in the *Domesday Book*, or marked on a Tudor map, you are doing rather well.

Post-1600AD, the classifications multiply; there are secondary and recent woodlands whose categories are subdivided into different classes. Further down the detailed list I found 'new native woodlands', located primarily on farmland.

Thus, Gorfenletch Wood was classified formally as a 'new native farm woodland of standards with coppice managed under CCF, commercial, amenity and wildlife interests'. At first, Elizabeth and I were unsure what to call the future Wood.

David's Wood was pretentious, and Parky's Plantation was appalling. Six Acre Wood would mislead if the woodland expanded. So Gorfenletch Wood it was, after the original farm. No toponymical anthology is complete without the 'gorse by the stream' and a novel, *The White Foxes of Gorfenletch*, was published in 1954. References.

I gazed at the empty field and considered tree planting. The undertaking included: preparing the site; marking out the tree positions with shelter stakes, hammering them in; applying herbicide; buying stock, preparing them for planting (trimming roots and feeble shoots); planting and attaching the shelters to the stakes; eight procedures per tree. I had thousands of them and the winter days were short.

The first four were late summer work and early autumn work. The site was mown in August allowing the cuttings to decay before spraying herbicide around the stakes in September. In October I would stock up with shelters leaving me free to collect and plant the saplings in winter.

A young tree requires a shelter to protect it from vermin [6] and each shelter has a stake to hold it upright. The cost of seven thousand shelters and stakes together equalled the cost of a deer fence.

There were plenty of deer present in the neighbourhood to justify a fence. The prospect of erecting a half-mile perimeter barrier, eight feet high with myriads of twelve-foot posts set into stony ground was the stuff of nightmares. The finished deer fence would not protect the trees from rabbits and limit woodland expansion opportunities. Shelters were easier, and I stuck with them.

I would begin planting small quantities of trees, and, after gaining experience, increase the daily amounts. Home was halfway between the nursery and the Wood, making sapling, shelters and stake [7] collection easier. I stored the trees in the garden shed and transported the daily planting quota to the Wood.

I made a note to service the van, replace my work boots and buy a tree planting spade. Quality counted, and only professional kit would suffice.

I finished my mug of tea, and, with a wood burning stove to install, went to fetch a tape measure from the van. I walked back over the field picturing a fully-grown wood; a startled pheasant broke my reverie.

Cold winter days of hard, repetitive outside work lay ahead. There was little reprieve in summer with weeding and mowing. Autumn would bring the failed sapling tally. Nature was boss, and my lofty reflections tempted fate. Establishing the Wood was not going to be easy. Undeterred, I turned my attention to the tree planting plan.

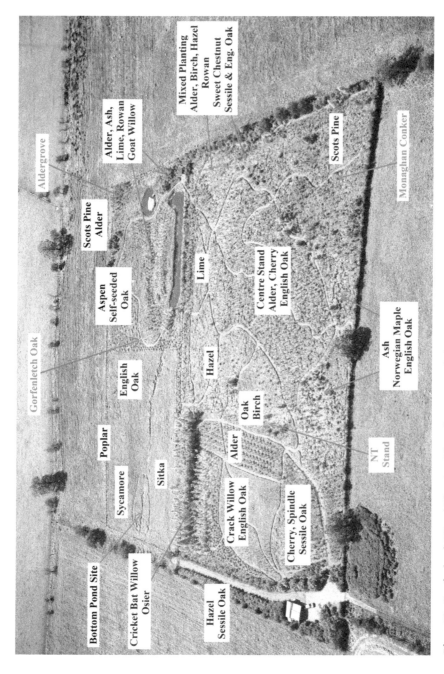

Plate 10. *Gorfenletch Wood Planting Plan.* ©*air images ltd.*

The following labels appear on the plan:

- Bottom Pond Site
- Cricket Bat Willow Osier
- Gorfenletch Oak
- Aldergrove
- Sycamore
- Poplar
- Sitka
- English Oak
- Aspen Self-seeded Oak
- Scots Pine Alder
- Alder, Ash, Lime, Rowan Goat Willow
- Mixed Planting Alder, Birch, Hazel Rowan Sweet Chestnut Sessile & Eng. Oak
- Hazel Sessile Oak
- Crack Willow English Oak
- Alder
- Oak Birch
- Hazel
- Lime
- Centre Stand Alder, Cherry English Oak
- Scots Pine
- Cherry, Spindle Sessile Oak
- NT Stand
- Ash Norwegian Maple English Oak
- Monaghan Conker

3 1

7

Sundials

It is easy to consider the oak as a British tree and forget how global the three hundred species of oak are. I wanted to know what defined a British native tree from the rest.

About eleven thousand years ago, the retreating glaciers were followed by the wildwood which was cleared one way or other by man. The naturally regenerating trees growing between the glacial retreat and man's clearances are the native trees of Britain. The original wildwood trees were identified by analysing ancient pollen samples.

Pollen grains are small, dense and numerous. They are distinctive to plant species and survive for thousands of years in soil. Pollen analysis of archaeological soil layers show the northern wildwood's dominant species comprised of alder, birch, elm, oak and pine. The understory—trees growing beneath the dominant's canopy—were aspen, black-thorn, cherries, crab apples, hawthorn, hazel, holly, rowan and spindle. Ash was present, and willows occupied the wetlands. These species are represented in the Wood and amongst others I included the native small leaf lime.

The lime, loved by bees, is beyond its natural range in Northumberland. There are impressive specimens at Wallington, and, inspired by the midland hawthorn, I decided to give lime a try. The light, fibrous wood was used for shields, and the bark processed like flax, spun into strong rope. Lime shields and rope have fallen into disuse and these properties remain. I speculated what other archaic commercial values lay in the woodland, and if the obsolete uses came back into fashion, so much the better for potential woodland worth.

Alder wood is light, used for clogs and the charcoal for gunpowder. The tree fixes nitrogen in the soil and grows on wet ground. It burns quickly making it useful for kindling.

Any tree can be firewood and the market has taken off over the last decade. As I manage the Wood for timber, I will always have firewood. Manage only for firewood and it is all you will get. The hardwoods, ash, hawthorn (ideal for old fashioned bread ovens) oak etc. are in high demand for stoves. Not so for the slow burning black poplar with shock absorbing qualities.

Back in the sixties, match manufacturers, who used the steady burning wood for their match sticks, were asking people to plant poplars to meet demand. The heat resistant qualities of poplar planks were used for floorboards around fireplaces and it was useful for machinery brake blocks. The shock absorbing characteristics were utilised for wagon floors and rifle stocks. I planted poplars for shelter belts and included hawthorn and blackthorn.

The two trees make spikey hedges especially when combined with dog and field rose. Gorse, whose early yellow flowers attract bumble bees, adds to the prickles. Honeysuckle gets everywhere, and the bright red berries of the guilder rose supplement autumn colour. There is always a space for holly.

Holly is better when planted in clumps for berries. It is said the orange pink fruits of the spindle tree once replaced holly berries at Christmas. The thornless spindle's hard wood was favoured for loom spindles and knitting needles.

Blackthorn produces sloes for sloe gin. Elder flowers, berries and birch sap are wine ingredients, whilst the Russians used rowan berries for the same thing. Crab apples make jelly, and hazelnut shells have been found in Iron Age excavations, proving the nut's abiding popularity as food.

The Iron Agers carved runes into rowan staves; the tree was reputed to ward off evil. The rowan is regarded as the sovereign protector of milk and the Irish planted it near dairies. The wood was made into spinning wheels for wool processing. The tree thrives on hillsides, where it is known as mountain ash. It is a different species than the familiar ash.

No wood can be without the ash tree and I rued the day I chose it. The young timber is flexible and is believed to have been used as chariot axle springs. It is the best firewood. The tree grows anywhere, and I have seen them growing on the walls of dilapidated buildings. Their canopy cover is light, in contrast to beech and yew.

I find the dense shade of those trees depressing, and, as paymaster general, I rejected them in favour of Scots pine and Sitka spruce. I find the ambiance of a decently thinned pine stand attractive and the timber is valuable.

Beside the pines, I value the oaks and cherries for their value as future saw logs. Hazel and willows could be coppice for quicker financial returns.

Hazel and osier willow stems are used for basket and hurdle manufacture. Their coppice rows make wind breaks when harvested rotationally. I was advised to plant several willow species as a defence against disease so included crack, goat and cricket bat willows.

CBWs are in demand and I dreamt of the winning Ashes run scored with a Gorfenletch bat. CBWs grow into substantial trees, rivalling oaks in stature. I went to look for large oaks and their acorns.

I found first-rate examples at Floors Castle, Roxburghshire and the Katherine Parr Oak, Yorkshire. I sowed them and half of them sprouted, increasing the Wood's gene pool. Our home bestowed four different young trees.

The garden donated a holly, a pair of ash and a Victoria plum. I was given a silver birch, horse chestnut, two dozen alder, an unidentified willow, an elder, and seventy sessile oaks.

The holly self-seeded underneath the back hedge and it seemed logical to transplant it in the Wood.

The two ash seeds rooted below a hydrangea and a rose bush. They were extracted and helped gap up a hedgerow. The Victoria plum attracted wasps and was exiled to a far corner of the Wood.

The silver birch was planted near the Woodland gate. The six-inch horse chestnut seedling came with a warning: the parent tree was colossal, and within six years the 'sapling' was fifteen feet high. The alders were planted in the north-west corner of the Woodland forming a small Aldergrove so named in appreciation of their donors, as was the Monaghan Conker.

A willow with grey bark, an elder tree and seventy oak seedlings were donated by Wallington Garden. The willow is flourishing between the Top and Long Ponds. The elder has settled nearby and every autumn is laden with berries for the birds. The oaks form the NT Stand and the species list pseudonym for the willow is in recognition of the gifts.

I dotted the wood with red oak, sweet chestnut and Wych elm. I am taken by the autumn colours of red oak, and sweet chestnut was a childhood favourite. I risked the disease prone elm. So far, they have not succumbed, whereas other trees I thought least likely to have. The irony was not lost on me; tree disease afflicted the Wood later and tested my resolve.

The previous pond site owner planted Scots pines, now an effective, pheasant-attracting wind break. The site is home to an increasing number of self-seeded oaks. The nearest mature sessile oak stands three hundred yards west of the Woodland and the random ground pattern of the seedlings indicates dispersal by birds. I shelter the young oaks and wonder if I should have left nature to establish the Wood. Maybe one day I will.

I stood by the 1866 ash as the November sunrise cast early shadows; once upon the wildwood and now the tree shelter stakes, their silhouettes sundials across the grass. It was time, no more would pasture prevail. I fetched the saplings from the van.

The trees were coming back.

8

The Trees Return

I planted and sheltered the first twenty-five hazels on Monday 8th November, 2002. My tree planting technique was undeveloped, and I was pleased my autumn preparations paid off. I went home happy, and over dinner, glasses were raised to the foundation of the Wood!

The compacted top soil was ripped in August. I set the stakes out in September and was careful not to place them on the rip lines. A drought the following summer would open the lines and expose the sapling roots.

I carried twelve stakes and stuck them by hand into the ground. After a couple of dozen or so, I checked and adjusted the layout, avoiding the rank and file look. When satisfied, I knocked them in with a stake driver, a tube welded shut at one end that slides over the stake to whack it into the ground.

(The stake driver is the blue device leaning against the background fence post in Plate 7. It is impossible to hit your hand or fingers when using it).

I used a knapsack sprayer to apply the herbicide around the stakes, preventing double spraying by shaving a top corner of the treated stake with a pruning knife. Woad, a blue vegetable dye, is now available from pesticide merchants to colour the herbicide solution making the sprayed areas easier to see. By October there was a square yard of dead grass around each stake and the ground was ready to plant.

Over the years my tree planting skills improved. I used a lightweight, fibreglass handled tree planting spade - its tapered blade making short work of the hole. I heard a lot of bluster over the shape of the hole. The hypotheses proposed an incongruous argument where the roots must benefit from a square hole after being grown in a round pot and vice-versa. I have yet to observe the cube-shaped root mass of a blown down tree and what happens to the roots of self-seeded trees?

I was digging over a hundred holes a day. There was little enough daylight to spend fussing over the shape of a hole especially when half of the short day was reserved for sheltering-up.

Tree roots have a symbiotic relationship with *mycorrhizae* fungi. The fungi help the roots absorb water and nutrients out of the soil. In return the tree supplies the fungi with sugars. Neither tree nor fungi would thrive without the other and neither are influenced by round or square holes.

The holes have to be deep and wide for two purposes: one, to allow the roots to follow their natural downward spread from the stem; two, to cover the roots with soil no more than an inch over the nursery soil line of bare-rooted saplings or the top of the root plug on cell grown stock.

Plate 11: Sitka saplings left; cell grown and right, bare-rooted. Deciduous roots are the same. Both root types grew satisfactorily in the Wood.

In practice, the inch of soil was the width of my gloved index finger. Small shoots up to the inch line were trimmed off as pre-planting preparation, or if short and skinny, ignored. The holes varied in size and shape enormously.

I found the shape of the hole related to soil condition. Digging into average top soil produced roundish holes or root pits. Wet soil demanded a different approach.

I drove the spade into the soil up to the top of the blade. I pulled it smartly back to open a slit in the ground sufficiently deep to bury the roots. I removed the spade and drove it again into the earth about six inches in front of the sapling. I levered the spade forward to press the soil home against the roots and firmed in with a foot. It was an efficient method and used to great effect on alders and Sitka's.

The saplings were the stars of the show and I resolved, almost fanatically, to plant them correctly. I recalled Machiavelli's *'the end justifies the means'*; now even he was having a say in the Wood! I finished the day's batch before attaching the mesh shelters to the stakes with a staple gun. [8]

It was difficult to plant and shelter the tree in one operation efficiently. I was breaking my planting rhythm by stopping to pick up the mesh and attach it to the stake. It was like holding a spade in one hand and a staple gun in the other. Progress was disappointing. I split the planting and sheltering into two separate operations and my daily totals increased significantly. Mesh shelters gave the trees protection and there were good results from them, but they did have their drawbacks.

The shelters were removed for weeding after extracting the staples [9] and pulling it over the tree. Weed roots grew into the base of the mesh requiring a spade to dig the shelter free. On fitting or refitting after weeding, the shelters do not seal effectively to the ground making the saplings vulnerable to voles.

In fact, one summer was marred by a vole plague. They were easy targets for the owls who perched on the tree shelters and dropped down onto their prey as it scurried past below. Despite the owls' best attentions, over four hundred saplings were ring barked by voles. Most trees recovered, the new shoots sprouting away from underneath the gnawed bark. I did not want more attacks and so sealed the shelters to the ground with soil. The approach was effective.

However, the drawback was a slower planting rate and later shelter removal with weed roots growing into the mesh. By then, six-inch plastic tube vole guards became available and positioned around the sapling before the shelter was fitted. Additional expenses arose.

The trees emerged from their shelters and the lowest side shoots were due pruning to help form straight trunk. [10.] The lowest shoots were entwined into the mesh and prevented me pulling the shelters off whole. I cut the shelters free rendering them useless. Many trees remained vulnerable to vermin and a new mesh tube was wrapped around their stems for protection.

Chalara, a fungal infection, was now attacking the ash. I was replacing the losses with different trees and decided to use tube type tree shelters.

The detailed design of tubes improved over the years, with rounded top rims to prevent the sapling chaffing against sharp edges, ventilation holes and re-usable ratchet ties for stake attachment. The tubes were easily removed for weeding, an effective barrier against herbicide overspray and automatically vole proof. As with the meshes, I planted the days' trees first before 'tubing-up'.

The tubed trees have a few years to grow before pruning and I do not think I will have to cut the tubes away; it is easy to undo the ties and slide them over the young side shoots inside. The Wood was filling up with plastic and I wanted rid of it.

Both types of shelter are intended to degrade in the sun, crumbling eventually to dust. The earliest shelters are now fifteen years old and show little sign of deterioration. I am forbidden to burn or bury them and accept their re-cycling costs reluctantly.

These affairs were absent when the glasses rose!

Plate 12: Tree Shelters Used in the Wood.

Top: Left: Mesh with vole guard. Right: tube.

Bottom: Left: Mesh tube on young oak. Right: Wide hedging shelter, with integral herbicide shield. See Chapter 9.

9

Wildlife

After the first hazels, I gapped up the hedgerows with hawthorn, black-thorn and field rose. The lengths of the hedgerows were grassy low banks and the remaining trees, guessing by the thickness of their hori-zontal trunks, were last laid many years ago.

With an eighteen-inch space between each plant and in two rows, gapping up a hedgerow was more intense than planting trees at six-foot intervals. Saplings were protected by rabbit shelters supported by a pair of bamboo canes. The shelters were attached to the canes with plastic ties.

I wanted to preserve the varied plant species growing on the banks and did not spray off with herbicide. I removed the turf on a tree by tree basis, re-burying the sod grass down under the roots. Fixing the shelters was monotonous; a cane driver, smaller version of the post driver, was essential to set the canes, and fitting the ties was fiddly. *See* Plate 12

I was lucky to complete seventy-five trees a day, it was usually fifty. Today, my efforts have been rewarded with a dense cattle proof hedge, a home to robins, sparrows and wrens.

Emboldened by my hedgerow work, I planted a dog rose hedge beside the bottom track with a normally spaced strip of oak and ash behind. I turned to pollard the remaining hawthorn trees on the south hedgerow bank.

I used a ladder and bow saw to cut the branches and gave myself a hernia. It was an unwelcome development, hailing an early end to my planting season.

The doctor confirmed the diagnosis and there was no alternative to an operation. I do not like hospitals and even less so when an overnight stay is involved. The surgeon diagnosed a 'sportsman's hernia'. I was flattered, saying I'd been nowhere near an arena for years and explained briefly how the injury happened. He smiled, and his cheerful countenance helped soothe my instinctive misgivings.

I woke up the morning after the operation feeling relieved to have survived. The surgeon was pleased and gave a prognosis for a full recovery. My ordeal was over, and I reached for the mobile. Within the hour Elizabeth liberated me and we were back home.

I was not worried over the early end to planting. No saplings were on order and tree planting-wise everything could wait until the autumn. I spent a leisurely fortnight organising the wild flower meadow.

I chose a south facing site overlooking the dog rose hedge. The contractor arrived and spent fifteen minutes tilling the field with his twelve-bladed plough. Scores of sea gulls followed the tractor feasting on the exposed earth worms. Three days later he returned to harrow and sow the two and a half stone (16kg) of wild flower seed mix.

In summer, the meadow was full of ox-eye daisies. Over the following years the buttercups invaded, reducing the daises to isolated clumps; the red campion, cowslips, field scabious and plantain migrated into the woodland. It was not what I expected. I reduced the meadow area with hollies, which, due to flooding to be described later, were replaced with alder and crack willow.

Every September for eleven years I mowed the meadow and removed the hay to reduce soil fertility. My efforts were ineffective and in 2015 I abandoned the project. I wondered why hay removal was failing and what was making the flowers spread into the wood.

I presumed the trees were absorbing nutrients, making the ground more suitable for wild flowers. I was advised to plough the field deeply to put the infertile subsoil on top. I read later that subsoil was formerly used as a fertiliser, perhaps explaining why the weeds went mad on the pond spoil heaps. Nature scattered the flowers differently than planned and I kicked the questions happily into touch.

I planted the meadow with English oak, noting the wild flowers were returning to the crack willow and the alder stands. One surprise was the appearance of wild orchids, whose seeds were not in the original wildflower mix.

The orchids continued spreading to the north boundary hedgerow, home to self-seeded fox gloves, a clump of native bluebells and barn owls.

I bought the bluebell bulbs taking care they were the English native *Hyacinthoides non-scripta*. These have white pollen; the Spanish variety have blue. Wire netting protects the clump from hares who nibble the early spring leaves. It will be a while before I have a bluebell wood.

Plate 13: ...the appearance of wild orchids.

Plate 14: Barn Owl Box with Sleepy Resident.

The Wood's north hedgerow gives way to grass where the barn owls hunt. I made a box for them and fastened it to a stout hawthorn tree. References

The owls were slow to adopt the box and crows were the first residents. I evicted them, cleaned out their mess of twigs and the owls moved in. Pairs of barn owls have occupied it since and raised several sets of owlets successfully. In winter, the red hawthorn berries attract fieldfares.

After the fieldfares depart, the hedgerows are busy with blackbirds, sparrows, finches and robins. The shrill song of curlews resonates across the fields, sky larks and cuckoos add their calls. A pair of swallows return in May to the containers' eves where they nest and raise two broods.

Plate 15: *Swallow Chicks under the Eves.*

Many more swallows find their way to the ponds, where they swoop over the water for insects. They share space with herons and oystercatchers. There are rare visits by hoopoes and shrikes. Ducks and geese are regular visitors, deer visit occasionally; there is abundant water for all.

The roe deer are the largest wild mammals seen in the Wood and the shelters protect the trees from them. Foxes keep hares on their toes as the weasels do for rabbits. Mice and voles are owl prey. I let the wild creatures be, enticing them only with ponds.

10

"The Aliens Have Landed!"

The preliminary idea for ponds arose when I saw the winter stream flowing past the Wood's west hedgerow. That site was bought shortly after mine and fenced off into a three-acre paddock. My pond plans faded until 2006 when the owner sold up.

I could not afford the whole price and shared the cost of the land with a friend. In 2012, I bought his half. In between, the Top and Long Ponds were excavated. The third, Bottom Pond, was added in 2013. The ponds were exciting projects involving excavators, piers, islands and planning permission. [11.]

The Top Pond was excavated first. I hired a mini-excavator and dumper. My friend was a fully trained excavator operator and I drove the dumper. Each mini-excavator bucketful was a decent wheel barrow load and the dumper took ten loads to fill. The four-wheel dumper was highly manoeuvrable, comfortable to operate and with one lever pull, a half-ton of earth was tipped effortlessly onto the spoil heap.

The excavator was steered and driven by its tracks. The steering is controlled by a pair of tillers. The left tiller brakes the left track effectively making it a pivot for the free running right track to turn the excavator left. Vice-versa for the right turn. Push both tillers simultaneously and the excavator moves forward, pull them both back for reverse.

The excavator's digging action mimics the human arm reaching out with a downward cupped hand and scooping up soil. I gave digging a go, imagining the excavator boom was my arm doing the work. Two different levers control the digging, and after a few practice scoops I loaded up the dumper without spillage. The pond was excavated in three days.

Plate 16: Long Pond.

The Top Pond is the smallest of the three. I was more ambitious with the second, the Long Pond, whose excavation was beyond my rudimentary digger skills. I saw a contractor producing high-quality work at Wallington and he agreed to work for me.

Contractors come as a package; there are no self-hire worries over fuel supply, machine insurance and cleaning. The tractor and trailer, with the twenty-ton weight excavator on board, trundled down the track to the woodland gate, and after unloading, the work began. The digger was an impressive machine, removing ten times more spoil per scoop than the mini-excavator.

There was no call for a dumper; the spoil was excavated and dumped in place with one swing of the excavator's boom. The excavator was powerful - a rock the size of a settee was disinterred and cast aside as if a box of feathers.

The work was finished in two days and I built an observation shed overlooking the entire length of the pond. As happens with sheds, the use changed to a tree shelter, post and stake store.

Three years later the Bottom Pond was excavated. I employed the same contractor, who arrived with a new twenty tonner. He excavated and landscaped the spoil around the pond circumference, finishing the job the morning before a woodland society visit. I showed my visitors the fresh hole.

"The aliens have landed!" pronounced an awestruck guest.

There was murmuring agreement as they beheld the dry crater. I prayed the aliens would not return to the full pond as invasive, non-native weed.

I built piers for the Top and Bottom Ponds using railway sleepers as stanchions preserved with creosote [12]. With helping hands and logging tongs, these were upended into three-foot deep holes and jammed vertically with stones before back filling with quick drying concrete. The beams for the Top Pond pier were scrounged from Wallington, and second hand square fence posts made the walkway. The bottom pier was more substantial using 4.8m (sixteen-foot) joists, pre-treated with preservative by the supplier. Its 2.4m width allowed economical use of the timber and the eight-foot planks for the deck. Easier written than done.

I saw the floating islands first in London. The derelict Surrey Docks were redeveloped, and the vast Greenland Dock preserved for

Plate 17: "The Aliens have landed"

Plate 18: Bottom Pond Pier.

Plate 19: Top Pond and Floating Island.

houseboats, water sports and wildlife. The floating islands were an addition to help the water fowl nest. The idea was successful, and I fancied a floating island for the Top Pond.

I contacted the manufacturers who told me the island came as a kit and I was in luck. The following day they were dispatching a quantity of islands to a wildlife reserve situated off the A1, thirty miles south of the Wood. They added my island to the cargo and delivered it to the Wood on the subsequent afternoon.

The island floats on four large-diametric, sealed plastic tubes, bolted together to form a square frame. A metal gird is attached to the frame which supports thick coir mats of pre-planted sedge grass.

The island is anchored to the pond bed with a heavy weight. I procured a fifty-gallon galvanised metal tank and cut a two-inch round hole in the bottom. I plugged the hole with a polythene bag and attached the anchor chain. Wearing waders, I floated the tank into position, pulled the bag out of hole and the tank began to fill with water.

The tank filled up. A gallon of water weighs ten pounds and this gave five hundred pounds (225kg) of anchorage. The tank went under sinking quickly and I was pleased my feet were well clear.

It was important to allow adequate slack on the anchor cable to allow for changes in the water level. I adjusted it twice, the successful attempt witnessed by the flock of bleating sheep. The sedge grass grew quickly, and the island is a home for nesting ducks.

The clay subsoil saved fitting artificial linings to the ponds. Taking Environment Agency advice to combat alien pond weed, I left the ponds to colonise naturally with aquatic plants. I planted native flag iris and reed mace for bankside cover. I was also notified birds may bring in fish eggs stuck to their feet. I held little hope for the migrant fish, Heronsclose Burn did not get its name for nothing.

The herons, ducks and geese make life difficult for amphibians. Frogs are seen occasionally; toads and newts are non-existent. Bankside and pond plants are flourishing so maybe the aquatic reptiles will gain a better chance.

The ponds followed the main field drain, running ran directly south to Heronsclose Burn. The secondary field drains were connected to the main pipe forming a herringbone pattern drainage system. All the ponds were excavated to below the main drain level. The clay pipes were removed, and the main drain sealed with clay where it left the ponds under the bank. The secondary pipes were left open and help maintain water levels after the winter stream dries up.

The Top and Long Ponds' drains were blocked successfully. The Bottom Pond's drain was set in rubble which proved difficult to seal, and in 2015 the Pond leaked dry.

I used the occasion to deepen the pond, using the excavated spoil to make the island.

It was a weekend job and I was surprised to hear jet engines; the RAF did not normally fly on Saturdays.

I looked skywards and saw the mighty Vulcan Bomber flying directly towards me. I waved, the plane dipped a wing and was gone, vanishing over the hilltop, the prodigious rumble of its four mighty Rolls-Royce Olympus engines fading in my ears.

Plate 20: Bottom Pond and Island.

I left the pond dry for a year to allow the island to settle, otherwise the water would dissolve the uncompact soil. In September, I blocked the drain with a quarter ton of puddled clay and thumped the stuff home with the blunt end of a four-inch fence post. A wet autumn week refilled the pond and the water level remained reassuringly steady.

The pond spoil heaps were landscaped and planted with goat willow, ash, rowan and Sitka. I'd seen young, unsheltered Sitka plantations with insignificant vermin damage. I followed suit and regretted it.

11

Woodland Weeds

The Sitka were attacked by hares who chewed the shoots off and abandoned them on the ground. The spruce needles turned pale - grass entwined itself amongst the trees preventing the use of herbicide. I resigned myself to hand weeding sessions when the needles returned to their original green and hare damage stopped.

I assumed the *mycorrhizae* fungi was re-establishing itself amongst the roots and the weeds, common grass and rush, barricaded the hares. The spruce showed no more signs of distress, many whips recuperated, and several stems are now six-foot high. I was pleased with the Sitka, not so the Scots pines.

The lure of owning a thousand new telegraph poles to sell was great. I planted an acre of Scots pine, protecting them with mesh shelters. The results did not go to plan.

The terminal buds were now clear of the shelters and safe from deer. I removed the shelters and the pines flopped to the ground. The needles were embedded into the mesh and supported the trees. In consequence, the roots developed inadequately and were unable to hold the pines upright. I tied the pines to the shelter stake; they began to recover, and I congratulated myself. The next winter, a blizzard broke the tree ties and the heavy snow bent the pines to the ground. My ambitions for a thousand telegraph poles were dashed.

I thinned out the damaged trees and removed the stakes. It was miserable work. The sun came out, cheering me up. The surviving pines would self-seed, and one day there shall be telegraph poles.

The pines thrived, curving upwards and straightening to grow into a wood of giant upside-down walking sticks. They nurse English oak saplings, protecting them from the worst of the weather. Woodland weeds, purple loose strife and yellow-flowered ragwort appeared, their flowers making an excellent display.

Weeds are plants growing where they are not wanted. In new woodlands they compete with saplings for light, nutrients and water, whilst also harbouring pests, such as slugs, for spite. The whips need regular weeding around and inside their shelters for two or three years. Canopy cover is the ultimate weed suppressor and until the joyful moment, woodland weed control is a reality. I declared war and assembled my arsenal.

The armoury fell into three sections; mechanical, the brush cutter and strimmer; chemical, herbicides applied by knapsack sprayer and weed-wiper; manual, tree planting spade, grubbing mattock, and leather gauntlets. *See Plate 7.*

The twenty-one horse-power, heavy duty, ride-on brush cutter makes quick work of mowing. It is a robust machine designed for woodland work. The strimmer is effective in clearing vegetation where the mower cannot reach. Be careful when strimming near trees!

Herbicide [13] is an efficient and economical way of weed control. I apply glyphosate for general woodland weeding and spot spray clopyralid on thistles with the knapsack sprayer. The weed wipe is excellent for treating weeds in awkward places, such as bindweed growing under hedges.

I labelled Woodland weeds as plants, except trees, not included in the wildflower meadow seed mix or interesting species like orchids, bluebells and fox gloves. The weeds fell into four groups, the first being those left alone; buttercups, dandelions, purple loose strife, rosebay willow herb and sedge type grasses.

The buttercups, taller than the garden variety, displace agricultural grass. Dandelions flower early attracting bumble bees fresh from hibernation. Purple loose strife and rose bay willow herb are bee friendly too. Sedge-type grass is my name for any wild grass similar to pampas in shape and habit. The remaining three groups are systematically destroyed and comprise of:

First, weeds inside and near tree shelters: all species. Second, perennial nuisances around the Woodland: bindweed, common rush, mare's tail and stinging nettles. And third, those covered in The Weeds Act 1959, which declares docks, ragwort and thistles as injurious to livestock and their spread must be controlled by the land user. I give no quarter to docks and thistles. I am more merciful towards ragwort.

The ragworts bright yellow flowers attract bees. After the bees finish and before the seeds ripen I uproot and burn the plants. Ragwort leaves are devoured by the black and yellow striped caterpillars of the cinnabar moth, presently unseen in the Woodland. The larvae's voracious appetite impressed the Americans, Australians and New Zealanders sufficiently to use the moth for ragwort control.

Plate 21: Ragwort and Bumble Bee.

I avoid spraying near desirable vegetation, preferring to hand weed the tree shelters, and, wearing leather gauntlets, pull up thistles growing amongst the wild flowers. The tree spade's tapered blade helps remove deeper rooted weeds and the grubbing mattock unearths isolated clumps of common rush with ease.

I experimented with mulch, which smothers weeds. Mulch takes many forms including proprietary matting, grass cuttings, wood chips and old carpets.

I used metre square woven plastic mulch mats to protect holly saplings. The weeds encroached quickly over the mats, their roots anchoring them firmly to the porous plastic sheet. I sprayed the weeds off knowing I could have done so in the first place. I removed the mats and gave them to a garden allotment association.

To be fair, act big with mulch; the greater the area and—within reason—the depth, the better. Voles live under mulch, so consider vole guards to protect the saplings.

I mow the tracks regularly, less so between the trees. The tracks are strewn occasionally with molehills. I scatter them with a shovel prior to mowing – if not the soil blunts the £80 per set swivelling cutting tips of the one metre long, forged steel, rotary blade.

I was mowing the Bottom Pond field when a kestrel followed me, hunting the voles fleeing from the machine. It returned six times catching a vole each trip before flying off towards a neighbouring wood. I imagined there were some fat kestrel chicks in the nest. The cutter is one of three machines I use around the Woodland.

I bought a track driven barrow to help carry tools and materials for Woodland maintenance. It has already proved value for money. I modified the loading bay to carry the wood chipper.

The chipper deals with the accumulation of brash and thinning in the Woodland, saving bonfires for diseased brash. I leave the chips as beetle breeding 'bio-heaps'.

The Woodland weeds are under control; on the other hand, different issues were generating their own troubles.

12

An Unanticipated Event

The water table level was rising across the old farm. A series of wet springs and summers prevented the winter rain water draining fully and parts of the Woodland were waterlogged.

I wanted to complete the centre stands with oak and cherry. The first batches were planted and now the ground resembled a paddy field. I changed the plan and stocked up with alder. The results look promising: the alder is drawing the oaks and cherries up, and the canopy is closing.

Earlier I planted the northern side of the wild flower meadow with hollies in five straight ranks to make berry collection easier. The stands were now sodden, and I moved the hollies to a drier spot. I replaced them with alder and crack willow. The planting plan was modified further.

There were mixed results with the two hazel coppices. The lower coppice grows between the main track and the south hedgerow, while the upper coppice lies further within the Woodland. The trackside and half the upper coppice were prospering, whilst the remainder of the upper coppice was waterlogged and stunted.

I let the stunted bushes be and thought the excessive water was leeching nutrients out of the soil. I planted downy birch and aspen, better suited to wet ground and their fallen leaves would add humus to the soil.

The main hazel coppice is exposed to the prevailing westerlies and one day will be sheltered by the Sitka spruce planted around the Bottom Pond. I will wait until the shelterbelt takes effect before redeveloping the coppice site.

My troubles with waterlogging were not over.

The elm, lime and rowan were inflicted with root rot. The worst cases died and were uprooted by hand. I left the healthy elms alone and transplanted the surviving rowans to the Long Pond spoil heap where they recovered. I coppiced a few limes leaving the strongest as standards. Both groups flourished, and a clump of standards has closed its canopy, an ideal spot to stand and daydream.

I call this 'creative contemplation', some may disagree, but I am the boss. Back in the root rot days, there was a sombre tone to my musings.

I accepted the Wood was at the mercy of the elements. The waterlogging, root rot and nutrient loss were unexpected. The Scots pine tragedy was a blow, doubtless there would be others. I was getting negative and snapped back; the pines were recovering were they not? The cloud lifted, and I turned my attention to the willows.

I planted cricket bat, osier and goat willows. My early dreams of Test cricket bats were postponed and there was limited demand for supplying osier to basket makers.

Cricket bats are made of straight grained, knot-free willow. The Wood's CBWs are exposed to gales; the seasoned wood is stressed and liable to split making it useless for bats. Knots are prevented by regular disbudding the trunk, a chore almost as labour intensive as processing osiers.

Osier stems are stripped of their bark and boiled before basket weaving. This meant investing in a de-barking machine and boiling tank, I preferred to spend the money on a brush cutter. The new CBWs would benefit from the improving shelter and keeping osiers to make baskets one day was better than not.

The willow coppices were held in reserve for future supply. They served as a continuous cover windbreak, each row coppiced every third year. If no use is found for the stems, they will be chipped and left in heaps to prevent individual chips growing into new trees. The future basket supply plan was not to be.

I had not anticipated the rising water table. I learnt where the new wet areas were and changed the tree planting accordingly. On my rounds, I observed the birch crowns were dying back with a fungal infection. The Wood was inflicted by tree disease and the consequences reverberate to this day.

13

Decimation

The silver birch crowns were dying back as they fell victim to either *Marssonina betulae* or *Anisogramma virgultorum*, fungal infections striking transplanted birch rather than self-seeded ones. Unhappily, the Woodland gate birch succumbed.

I cut the infected trees back and burnt the brash. I left the stumps alone and a few grew into healthy multi-stemmed trees. I restocked with downy birch and wait to see if the fungi attack them. My encounters with tree diseases were not over - oak mildew and other maladies were waiting in the wings.

The oaks were attacked by the fungus *Microsphaerea alphitoides*, the mildew whitewashing the leaves. The fungi struck young oaks in particular and the post-pruning growth of older trees occasionally. It was more common after cold springs, but all the oaks recovered without treatment.

In 2012, my mutterings about the cold spring were not allayed by the news of an ash tree killing disease in East Anglia. The chalara ash die back, abbreviated to 'chalara' or 'ash die back' (ADB) era was underway.

The disease is caused by the fungus *Hymenoscyphus fraxineus*, originally labelled *Chalara fraxinea*, and there was a national debate on how it arrived in the UK. My facts were plain; there was a virulent ash killer on home soil which was spreading northwards and I owned nine hundred young ash.

My ash were under twelve years old and susceptible to the disease. I faced a huge potential loss and monitored the trees over two summers. I saw no signs of the brown tips on the branches, the wilting leaves or the diamond-shaped stains on the trunks. By autumn 2013, I thought the Wood was safe; I was wrong. In 2014, the disease struck, and the ash were badly infected.

Plate 22: Ash Die Back. Right Inset: Typical external and internal staining.

I was reluctant to clear all the ash; it was bad enough dealing with birch and root rot. I had nothing to lose by pruning the infected branches off the larger trees hoping this would curtail the disease. Most of the branches were above head height and I bought a telescopic pole saw for the work.

I sawed the branches back to the main trunk. If there was no brown discolouration in the cut, the disease may not have entered the trunk and the disfigured ash might survive. Any infected trunks were cut back to a clean stump and left to sprout. I burnt the blighted wood.

Stump regrowth was vigorous and infected. Chalara had a firm grip on the newest saplings too and both would die before long. I cut both to ground level and with a paint brush applied a ten percent herbicide solution; there were wildflowers nearby and I was not taking chances with glyphosate spray drift.

I ran regular chalara patrols, pruning off freshly diseased branches, stumping and burning where necessary. The surviving trees were recovering their shape and the seasons would tell whether the disease was controlled in the Woodland.

The two ash in the east hedgerow showed no traces of ADB. The veteran was recovering from a lightning strike, and in frivolous moments I advocate lightening as a chalara cure.

I was taken aback by the scale and ferocity of ADB. The ash trees were planted between 2003 and 2013, came from different suppliers, and saplings grown from chalara-free Irish ash keys. The disease infected all, no sapling was immune, and no fungicide was available to curb it.

ADB is a continuing Woodland catastrophe. I replenished fatalities with English oak and Norway maple. I substituted ash with sycamore for the new stand west of the Bottom Pond.

By spring 2017, most of the ash were infected. It was obvious the pruning was not working. The trees were growing vigorously - the leaves hiding the dead branches making the trees look 'normal'. I changed my tactics.

I disregard ADB and cut the tree down when the disease becomes obvious. I am restocking with walnuts as an experiment and self-seeded oaks transplanted from other parts of the wood. My worries continued as ADB was running alongside two other inflictions.

I saw the first on my travels around Northumberland. The willow tree leaves were looking slightly brown and it was the same back at the

Wood. *Melampsora medusae,* or willow rust fungus, was infecting the goat willows and secondly the osiers.

All the goat willows were infected, their bright green leaves turning rusty brown with fungal growths not dissimilar in shape to the serpent infested head of Medusa. I eliminated the goat willows from the Wood, burning the brash and treating their stumps as per the ash. The main goat willow stands, the Woodland gate area and the Top Pond spoil heap were re-stocked with small leaf lime and Sitka spruce.

By summer 2017, the osiers succumbed and followed the goat willows to the bonfire. The basket supply plan was no longer. I decided to replace the osiers with standards for saw logs and chose wild cherry, *Prunus avium.* The CBWs and crack willows remain healthy. I am pleased I heeded advice to plant more than one willow variety.

*Plate 23: Tortrix Moth cobwebs
festooning a Bird Cherry.*

The second menace was Tortrix moth.

The moth attacked the spindles and bird cherries, *Prunus padus*. The moth lays eggs in a cocoon spun around the budding twigs, where the caterpillars hatch to strip the tree of leaves. The bird cherries were covered completely for several springs and did not recover from the repeated defoliations. I dealt with them in the usual manner and gapped-up with English oak. The spindles were less severely infected.

It was tedious work snipping the cocoons off the spindles. The trees remained healthy and I asked a pesticide merchant if there was a better way of controlling the moth. He said if the moth was flying there was little to be done, it was best to control the caterpillars. He offered a biological insecticide, 'biocide', as a solution to the problem.

The insecticide is based on the naturally occurring soil bacteria *Bacillus thuringiensis*. When the caterpillars eat the sprayed foliage, the bacteria cause the larvae to starve and fall off the plant. The bacteria are harmless to birds and beneficial insects. I bought a half kilo container of them and a new spray gun. I prepared for germ warfare.

In May the moth attacked, and the spindles were laden with cocoons of caterpillars. I mixed the brown powder, dormant germs, and water together, pouring it into the sprayer. The smell was similar to a dung heap. It was a calm day and I sprayed all the spindles and the few remaining bird cherries. I wore with full face protection and disposable coveralls. Chemicals are one thing, organisms bred to stop creatures eating are another.

The results were lethal for the caterpillars who starved and fell off the leaves. Both tree species recovered, and the spindles carried a heavy crop of berries.

The replacement birch, lime, maples, oaks and Sitka came away nicely. The sycamore have been slower, and after three years many have not reached the top of their shelters. I find the tree pleasant; the timber is valuable and plan to underplant them with hazel.

The Wood suffered many tree losses and I wanted to measure the extra impact disease was having on the Wood.

Beating up, the replacement of failed saplings, comes with woodland planting. I counted the first year's failures in August. I assumed the saplings were healthy when planted and should have shown some growth.

The disease and root rot numbers were recorded as they were discovered throughout the growing season. The two figures were recorded separately and combined for annual sapling replacement requirements.

Between 2002 and autumn 2016, thirteen thousand saplings were planted. Six percent, seven hundred and eighty, perished in their first year. One thousand six hundred and seventy-five died from disease over the same period, raising the total score to just under nineteen percent. The disease casualties by species were: five hundred ash, two hundred and fifty bird cherries, six hundred birch and seventy-five goat willows. Wild cherry, lime, rowan and elm (root rot, not the Dutch disease) accounted for two hundred and fifty.

By July 2017, five hundred osiers were infected with *Melampsora* and ADB was rampant amongst the remaining four hundred ash. When these are taken into account the total rises to just under twenty-six percent. Subtracting the first year loses, a fifth of the trees have yielded to disease.

I am stoical in the face of tree diseases - there is not much more to do than carry on. I have the odd 'chainsaw moment' when my discontent boils briefly over and I threaten to clear fell the whole Wood. After all, I am human, but of course I never will!

Fresh perils, oak processionary moth and grey squirrels, loom. The oak moths' caterpillars are repelled by the same anti-tortrix germs, so I am ready for them. I will cross the grey squirrel bridge when I come to it. Lurking abroad are the pathogens *Xylella fastidiosa* which, if ashore, would slaughter oaks, and *Neonectria nemacrospora* a canker lethal to firs, *Abies*. I am informed the Government is tightening import controls to prevent their entrance into the UK.

I began clearing the osiers with the chainsaw, poisoning the stumps with herbicide as I went along. The osiers were between ten and thirteen years old and had given me good coppice crops, which I donated to Wallington for willow hurdles. I bought one hundred and fifty wild cherries as replacements.

I lit the bonfire; the red-tipped yellow flames dancing across the diseased branches, crumbling to white hot embers below. The intense smokeless heat distorted the air above and within the shimmering haze soared Phoenix - the implacable, indomitable spirit of the Wood.

14

Moving On

It was the perfect winter day for replacing the osiers. The overnight clouds were clearing, and the sun shone down on frost free ground. I set the stakes the day before, and by noon the cherry saplings were planted. I would fit the tube shelters after lunch.

I arrived before dawn. I lit the gas lamps and the wood fuel stove - the lamps hissing gently as the kindling ignited the logs. The wood burner was the second stove fitted into the container; I was supposed to have installed it years ago.

Alas, temptation came in the form of a narrowboat coal burning range. I could not resist buying it, and my wood burning principles went up the chimney. The range served for eleven winters and the oven baked pizzas superbly. It was awkward to clean, and soot rusted through the cheap enamel flue pipes. My niece was restoring a barge, and, in the end, the range went back to its proper place.

I filled the lunch time kettle, remembering the day when I measured up to fit the inside container tap from the trough supply. I looked over a field then and today the view was trees. Despite disease, waterlogging and the extra expense they caused, the Wood was in good heart and as uneven aged as it could be.

Physically, my knees have not collapsed, and the steady exercise of Woodland activity has kept me in good shape. The Wood retains my optimism, absorbing my attention without being obsessive; I am a happy fellow.

I returned to the tube shelters. The plastic ties made their fitting easy and I finished early. I packed up and drove home to a hot tub. It was a worthwhile day, others were not so productive.

I promised myself Woodland working hours would be flexible and tried to avoid working in the rain or snow. The Northumbrian weather held different ideas.

Frequently, a glorious morning turned into an inclement afternoon with the westerly breeze accelerating to a gale. I liked to finish the daily tree quota and flouted the elements to finish the job, wet and triumphant. Decades ago I was told these hardships were character forming; I agree, especially when having a cosy lie-in and watching the sleet lashing against the bedroom window.

I am an early riser. In summer, I drive to the Wood in broad daylight and in winter it is headlamps all the way. Winter work was mostly planting, but is now giving way more to pruning the timber trees.

The Wood has no formal management plan until I apply for a felling licence, an operation still many years away. I record events in my *Chronicles of Gorfenletch Wood,* an easy-going journal evolved from the police pocket notebook days.

The seasonal rounds of sapling replacement, weeding, mowing and pruning continue; machines are serviced, tools, sheds, gates and fences maintained. A Woodland character is emerging. Neighbouring landmarks are no longer visible through the trees, and autumn leaves accumulate on the tracks. Canopy cover is progressing steadily.

Corners of the Wood, particularly near the hedgerows have closed the canopy completely. The Scots pines are almost there. The 'nursed' English oak between them are thriving, growing straight for their place in the sun. The purple loose strife and ragwort have disappeared. Elsewhere, cover is patchy, areas of open ground dominated by wildflowers remain.

An increasing number of trees are growing out of their mesh tube shelters, shedding them as snakes their skin. As the trunk expands, and becomes vermin proof, the tubes open to a point where strong winds blow them off the tree. The discarded tubes are gathered up as an after-gale Woodland task.

Rather than uprooting trees, the gales blew taller than average specimens in wetter ground downwards, leaving the roots loose in the soil and the stem at an angle to the ground. I used heavy duty posts and tree ties support the distressed trees, knocking the posts in with a large sledge hammer. Next was the hard bit, helping hands might be needed, as the tree was pushed up towards the post and supported as the tie was attached. The soil around the roots was firmed in by feet.

The trees recovered within three years or so, after which the ties were hopelessly brittle, and the treated stakes snapped off at ground level. Tree shelter stakes were broken occasionally by the wind too, clumsy mowing accounted for more. Murphy's Law applies to posts, stakes and ties; if they are none on site, there is wind and mower damage, or if they are in stock, there is not.

On a more pragmatic note, my worries over the new ditch beside Moorhen Plantation affecting the winter stream were unwarranted, and all the ponds water levels remain steady.

I am slightly perplexed by the ponds as they were not part of my original Woodland plan. I seized the opportunity to excavate them and changed a small part of the county forever. Was I evoking the presence of the great Northumbrian Capability Brown and what landscapes would he have created with modern earth moving machinery?

The Top and Long Ponds have settled with pond plants keeping the water clear. The Bottom Pond is recovering from its empty year and ducks with their chicks take shelter amongst the fast- growing reeds. The island is colonising with rosebay willow herb and wild grass.

The wild flowers flourish. The red campion has established itself amongst the dog rose hedge and the bluebells have given their best display to date. Barn owls occupied their box and raised another brood of two. By July fifteen, jay-dropped acorns germinated, the new trees for ash replacement.

Plate 24: Campion.

In, 2009 a seven-year-old Woodland grown oak in a sunny spot produced two acorns. Elizabeth planted them, with due ceremony, southwest of the Long Pond. The following spring one sprouted; Gorfenletch Wood was beginning to re-generate itself.

The seedling led an uneventful first year. It was sheltered, vole guarded and weeded. It shed its leaves in autumn and was ignored over winter. Spring 2011 saw new buds, and all was fine until 4th May when my chronical records:

"Two steps forward…one step back. Gorfenletch Oak acorn zapped by latish frost. May survive".

It did, growing three stems, and a year later I pruned the shortest two off. In 2017, I removed the shelter and wrapped a mesh tube around the lower trunk of the seven-foot high oak. Stepping back, I checked my work and looked to the horizon.

I saw Northumberland stretching between the misty Pennines and the pale blue North Sea. I looked west towards Wallington, invisible by distance, and remembered my madcap notion. The whim was now the Wood; I achieved what I had dared dream and turned to face the trees. Only they choose to grow, and for that I am sincerely thankful.

Plate 25: *The Gorfenletch Oak.*

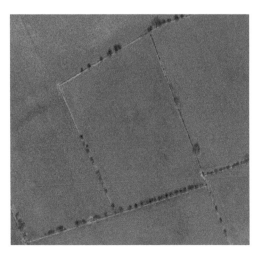

Plate 26: The field before the Wood c.1990. ©air images ltd.

Plate 27: The Wood 2007. ©air images ltd. The white area was freshly cut wet grass bleached dry by the sun.

Plate 28: Full size with Top and Long Ponds 2012. ©air images ltd.

Plate 29: Only the trees choose to grow… The Wood, July 2017. © air images ltd.

15

Notes

1: Containers

Containers are instant 20ft×8ft×8ft (6m×2.4m×2.4m) sheds. Other sizes are available. Most are sold second hand. Check for rust, dents, holes and paintwork.

It is important the outward opening doors are a snug fit into the frame, the hinges are free and the locking bars straight. Beware if angle iron hinge bolts are fitted. They are fixed to the inside of the outward opening doors and when open the bottom pair protrude at shin height above the ground.

Check with the supplier about delivery and access. Ensure there is ample space for the driver to turn the truck around and unload using the truck's jib. The lifting zone has to be clear of overhead cables, trees, branches etc.

A concrete slab foundation is ideal. If railway sleepers or similar are used, ways must be found of keeping vermin and moles out from underneath the container floor.

The floors are three quarter inch (19mm) thick plywood and should have no soft spots. They are replaceable; be prepared to deal with rusty screws and handle the full size 8ft×4ft (2.4m×1.2m) sheets.

When cutting new holes for windows and doors, 'nibble' out the waste metal sheet in smallish pieces, if not the waste sheet will spring free with considerable force.

The sides and corners may be slightly out of true making fitting out awkward. Assume there are no right angles and take loads of measurements.

2: Stoves

Stoves, flue pipes and accessories are readily available. Shop around for deals. Fitting stoves and flues are within the scope of a competent DIYer. Follow the manufacturer's instructions on stove and flue pipe fitting.

Consider having the flue coming out of a side wall – it will be easier to waterproof than the flue pipe exiting through the roof.

Flues can be tall structures and might require steel guy ropes for support.

An H-shape flue cowl prevents down-draught. If the stove does not have a damper a separate damper unit can be obtained to fit into flue pipes.

3: Hardstanding

Like a house foundation, it is best to lay hardstanding onto subsoil. If this is not possible spray off the surface vegetation with herbicide and compact the topsoil with a roller. Lay a propylene 'weed suppressant membrane' sheet over the surface before covering it with road planings, crushed rubble - stone chippings etc. Be wary of cheap rubble, it carries rubbish. Spray the hardstanding area in spring with a residual herbicide.

4: Establishment

Trees are established when they are no longer affected by weeds, early nutrient insufficiency and vermin. A wood is established when its trees close the canopy.

5: Coppice and Pollards

Coppice is a traditional way of utilising broad-leaved trees. The trees are cut back to stumps or stools. These are left to grow and after several years the multiple stems are harvested as poles. The process is repeated regularly, the years between harvesting referred to as 'coppice rotation' or 'coppice cycle'.

Coppice stands are usually divided into areas, the number matching the rotation period. A coppice with a five-year rotation has five areas, each cut annually in turn so after five years the cycle returns to the first area cut.

The rotation period depends on what uses the poles have. Willows for wickerwork will have a shorter rotation than hazels for hurdles.

Coppice shoots are vulnerable to vermin and the tree can be pollarded.

Pollarding is coppicing trees above human head height. The pruned-off branches leave a plain trunk enabling the new growth to sprout safely above the browsing lines of ruminants.

Regularly pollarded and coppiced trees can live for centuries.

6: Vermin

These are tree eating mammals. The main villains are: deer (all species), hares, rabbits, voles and grey squirrels. Tree shelters provide protection except for squirrels who are culled by shooting and trapping. There is on-going research to develop an oral contraceptive specific to grey squirrels. If successful it could be available within six to eight years.

7: Saplings and Stakes for Tree Shelters.

Wholesale rates for saplings, stakes and shelters usually apply. Saplings are sold as either cell grown, CG, or bare rooted, BR, stock. *See* Plate 11 CGs come in packs of ten wrapped in plastic film and delivered in boxes. BRs arrive in bundles of twenty-five, tied together with string and packed upright into strong, opaque, plastic bags. For sapling sizes please refer to the nursery catalogues.

On delivery open the boxes or bags to check the stock. CGs lie flat in their boxes and like BRs must be stored upright in their packaging. Count the saplings. Trim off any shoots less than an inch above the soil line and on BRs overlong roots. Keep all roots moist until planting and protect from frost. If planting is postponed heel in the BRs, there is no need to do this with CGs.

Dig a trench deep enough to cover the roots thoroughly. Lay the sapling bundles into the trench, their stems at an angle to the ground and thoroughly bury the roots. Cover the bare soil with straw or old plywood sheets for extra frost protection.

Rectangular, pointed shelter stakes are sold in bales of twenty-five as rot resistant hard wood or treated softwood. Hardwood stakes are largely knot free and can split lengthways, softwood's weak points are around the knots. Both can be wet and heavy after open air storage.

The stake length depends on the tree shelter used. When hammered into the earth the stake should be firm leaving sufficient length above ground to fix the shelter securely.

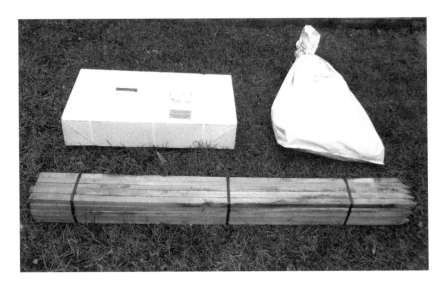

Plate 30: Saplings and Stakes as Delivered.

Plate 31: Sapling Bundles. Left: Cell grown. Right: Bare Rooted

I used 1.5m stakes driven into clay for 1.2m shelters.

Hold reserve stakes in case of wind and brush cutter collision breakages.

Bamboo canes are used to support shorter, wider shelters for hedging and fast-growing shrubs. The canes are banged into the ground with a cane driver, a smaller version of the post knocker without handles. The shelter is attached to the canes with non-releasable cable ties. *See* Plate 12.

Tree shelters are made from mesh or tube and come in various lengths, widths and profiles. Shelters for red deer are 1.8m long and for voles 0.2m, with hares, rabbits and roe deer falling between.

Mesh shelters are slippery to handle, and the top and bottom edges are sharp. The square profile varieties are sold in flat packs and have to be pulled into shape before fitting. Mesh tubes sold with five or more rolled up together and plastic tubes are sold with four tubes inside a fifth. Take care when unrolling or removing individual tubes.

When fitting mesh shelters use five feet of three-inch plastic pipe to prevent the mesh snagging the sapling. If using hedge shelters with herbicide shields, use two feet of four-inch pipe or similar.

Place the pipe upright over the sapling taking care not to dislodge the vole guard. Slide the mesh over the pipe. Apply staples and remove the pipe. My mesh guards and pipe were black, a disadvantage in fading winter daylight.

Wrap white insulating tape around the top of the pipe to assist visibility. What's more it keeps the muddy pipe bottom away from your hands.

8: Planting Notes:

1: A wheelbarrow is handy.
2: Prior to tree planting, give the stakes an extra hammer knock and place the shelters next to them ready for fitting.
3: Experiment how many trees can be planted and sheltered comfortably in a day, the number increases with practice.
4: Treat saplings respectfully, do not throw the bags or boxes around.
5: Whilst planting BRs, keep the roots moist by leaving the saplings in the bag. Even in winter the sun and wind can dry exposed roots quickly.

Mesh Shelter Fitting

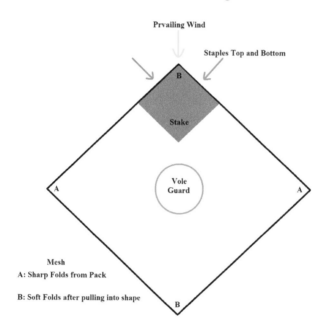

Plate 32: Mesh Shelter Fitting, theory.

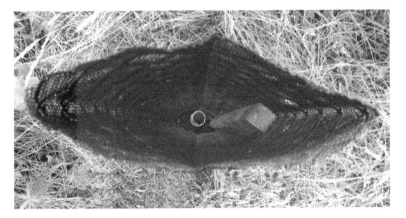

Plate 33: Mesh Shelter Fitting, field study.

Left; mesh guard, vole guard around seedling and stake.
Centre; Pipe fitted over vole guard. This allows the mesh to be slid over the stake and sapling without snagging sapling side shoots.
Right; mesh in place ready for stapling onto stake.
Top; Looking down, self-seeded oak protected by vole guard and mesh shelter.

6: Use the wheelbarrow as a mobile sub-depot for CGs and fill a bucket with unwrapped plugs. This saves moving the barrow from stake to stake. BRs can be carried in their bag up to the planting point.

7: Plant the tree a couple of finger widths away from the stake. If using mesh, keep the stake between the sapling and the prevailing wind so it can push the mesh onto the stake.

8: Push tubular guards an inch into the ground for a vole proof seal.

9: Staples occasionally jam in the gun. Carry the tools to clear the jam in a bucket. Fix the gun in the bucket, it saves parts falling into the mud.

10: Tubes use re-usable ratchet ties to attach them to the stakes. Take care not to strangle the sapling between the tie and the inside of the tube.

9: Removing Staples

I use the anvil blade tip of my Felco Model 7 secateurs to pry the soft iron staple out of the wooden stake. The secateurs are eighteen years old, the anvil shows no signs of wear and the tool continues to give a clean cut.

10: Formative Pruning

This is the removal of side shoots and branches to allow the tree to grow straight and produce a knot-free trunk for timber production. It is a winter job, except for cherries which are pruned in June to allow the wound to harden off. I pruned initially to above head height and over the years will progressively prune the side shots to twenty feet above the ground. Little and regularly is the trick, my best stems are presently twelve feet high.

11: Planning Permission

Tree planting and restoring neglected or infilled ponds are exempt from all planning regulations. Under the Town and County Planning Acts, excavating ponds requires formal planning permission. The application includes pond plans that must be drawn to professional standards.

The Acts also authorise the General Permitted Development Order. This details when planning consent is not required for certain developments.

Part 4 of the Order allows for the temporary use of the land for any purpose for up to 28 days in any one calendar year. This means you can live in your wood for four weeks a year.

Part 6 of the Order allows for *non-residential* buildings within woodlands. The local authority planners must be informed of your intentions and might place conditions on the development.

It is extremely unlikely you will be granted permission for a residential house on your woodland. Buying a house with land attached to plant a wood is probably an easier option.

Discuss your woodland, pond and building projects with your local planning department before submitting your application.

Planning application is now all on-line. See References for web site address.

Ensure you have the written permit in your hands before any work starts.

12: Railway Sleepers and Creosote

The standard railway sleeper is a nominal 8ft x10"x 8" (2.4m x 250mm x200mm). Longer and shorter lengths are available. They are made of either hard or soft wood and are sold new or reclaimed.

Reclaimed sleepers are graded from 'almost unused' to 'not quite firewood'. In general, reclaimed sleepers come with irregular profiles and rail attaching screws. All railway sleepers have splinters.

When handling sleepers, use work gloves. The sleepers weigh no less than a hundredweight (50kg) so have help on hand. Logging tongs are recommended. *See* Plate 9.

Softwood sleepers are usually preserved with creosote. Creosote is not allowed for use in areas in regular contact with humans such as playgrounds, outside tables and benches. It is forbidden absolutely in dwellings. Creosote is the best for underground and underwater wood-work and can be bought lawfully from agricultural merchants. Go for the twenty litre plastic bottles, some containers are made of thin, easily punctured metal sheet.

13: Chainsaws and Herbicides

Agricultural colleges run training courses on how to use both safely. My chainsaw courses were held under the Lantra (*LANd TRAining*) awards scheme, whilst my pesticide application, PA, courses were City and Guilds qualifications. They were expensive but what price is a chopped off foot or pesticide poisoning?

The chainsaw primer course covers maintenance and basic cross cutting techniques. This qualifies you to service the saw, sharpen the chain and cut logs to size. The second stage qualification is basic felling techniques for trees up to 8inches (200mm) in diameter. Here my train-ing stopped; my qualifications were satisfactory for everyday woodland work. The training courses progress to large tree felling techniques and tree climbing, using ropes, for height reduction and high branch pruning.

Buy a good quality chainsaw and safety wear from a reputable dealer used by foresters, arboriculturists, farmers etc.

There are twelve pesticide application training courses. The three most common are; PA1 the foundation course for the remaining eleven; PA2 machine and trailer mounted sprayers; PA6 for hand held applicators such as knapsack sprayers. I hold PA1 and 6.

Grandfather's rights, allowing unqualified use of pesticides for those born before 31st December 1964, were abolished in 2015.

If you use your chainsaw and PA qualifications professionally or voluntarily for charity, the liability insurers demand you attend refresher courses every five years.

Herbicide is the name for herbaceous plant-killing pesticide. Domestic use weed killers can be bought and used by all adults. Any adult can buy industrial strength, professional use herbicides. The merchant will ask you to ensure the end user is qualified to apply them.

Glyphosate is a non-residual and non-selective. It is sold widely under different brand names. Clopyralid is residual, does not kill grass and is faster acting than glyphosate.

DiPel® is the trade name for the insecticide I used to kill the caterpillars.

Soft water is best for mixing pesticide solutions. Water softening agents are available from pesticide merchants. Consider collecting rainwater, the larger the water barrel the better.

References:

Aerial Photography:
Air images Ltd: www.aerialphotography.com
Nunsbrough House, Hexhamshire, N'bria, NE46 1SY

Bibliography:
Available Forestry Commission Publications: www.forestry.gov.uk
Establishing Farm Woodlands, Handbook 8.
The Creation of Small Woodlands on Farms, Forestry Commission Scotland.
Creating New Native Woodlands, Bulletin 112.
The Silviculture and Management of Coppice Woodlands.
Utilisation of Hazel Coppice, Bulletin 27.
These are technical books whose titles are self-explanatory. They are invaluable reference guides on how to establish a woodland.
The frontispiece of *Bulletin 27*, published 1956, is paper made from hazel wood pulp. The FC supply a high quality, ring bound photocopy of the original.

A Glossary of Tree Terms, the Royal Forestry Society.
Top rate forestry jargon buster. Obtainable directly from the Society, no need to be a member.

The History of the Countryside, Phoenix Press and *Woodlands*, Collins.
Two must read tomes by the late, respected academic Dr Oliver Rackham.

The New Book of Apples, Joan Morgan and Alison Richards. Ebury Press, London.
Orchards are a woodland specialism. This beautifully illustrated book is the defining guide to apples listing over two thousand varieties. It includes the history of apple cultivation, the story of cider with informative appendices on cooking the fruit and growing the trees.

A Photographic Guide to Trees of Britain and Europe, Paul Sterry and Bob Press. Connaught.

Takes over form the classic Observers book series. Pocket size with colour plates.

Out of Print:
Flora of Northumberland, George A. Swan. The Natural History Society of Northumbria.
The Observer's Book of Trees. Frederick Warne & Co Ltd.
Trees and Their Life Histories, Percy Groom. Cassell & Company Ltd 1907.

Professor Swan's *Flora* lists the plant and tree species growing in Northumberland. I grew up with the latter two.

Book Reviews:

The Man who Planted Trees, Jean Giono. Far Far Away Books.

This is a short story of how a shepherd reforested a barren region of France, restoring hope and pride to the local inhabitants.

The region was deforested by charcoal burners. Streams and wells dried up, villages depopulated and houses fell into ruins. For years the shepherd collected and planted acorns widely across the countryside. Thanks to his efforts the landscape regained its original vitality.

The White Foxes of Gorfenletch, Henry Tegner. Hollis and Carter 1954.

In 1949, the Royal Zoological Society of Scotland recorded an outbreak of albinism in foxes living in the Cheviot Hills. Henry Tegner used this unusual occurrence as the basis of his novel.

White Foxes... is a huntin', shootin', fishin' yarn telling of spooky goings-on in the Northumbrian foothills of the Cheviots. It is also a cautionary tale against those who unwisely fell trees.

Gorfenletch is the name given to moorland traversed by a disused coach road. The abandoned highway climbs over the moorland and past trees nearby the ruins of an ancient inn of murderous repute.

White foxes materialise, horses refuse their mounts and loggers meet their untimely demise.

The white foxes remain to be seen in the Woodland.

Editorial: www.debzhobbs-wyatt.co.uk

Floating Islands: www.verdantsolutions.ltd.uk

Owl Box Construction Plans: *Garden Woodwork,* Richard Blizzard. Ward Lock.

The Barn Owl Trust: www.barnowltrust.org.uk

RSPB: www.rspb.org.uk

Northumberland County Archives: www.experiencewoodhorn.com

Nurseries for trees:

Cheviot Trees, www.cheviot-trees.co.uk

Newton Brae, Foulden, Berwick-upon-Tweed, TD15 1UL

Trees Please, www.treesplease.co.uk

Dilston Haugh Farm, Corbridge, Northumberland, NE45 5QY

Planning Permission: Planning Portal; www.planningportal.co.uk

Ponds:

Pond creation; www.freshwaterhabitats.org.uk

Pond restoration; Please Google the Aquatic Restoration Partnership.

Wallington Hall: www.nationaltrust.org/wallington

Wilson's Letter of Complaint: *See* Plate 34.

Woodland Societies:

It would be unfair to judge which society is best and all are highly recommended to anyone who is interested in and wants to be involved with trees. All the societies are passionate about woodland education, promoting the importance of trees to us and succeeding generations.

Each organizes woodland events and keep members up to date with high quality magazines and websites.

The Royal Forestry Society, www.rfs.org.uk

The Hay Barns, Home Farm Drive, Banbury, OX15 6HU

Small Woods, www.smallwoods.org.uk

Station Rd, Coalbrookdale, Telford, TF8 7DR

Woodlands Trust, www.woodlandstrust.org.uk

Kempton Way, Grantham. Lincolnshire, NG31 6LL

Telegrams:
Möller, Newcastle.
Telephones:
National – N°1303.
" " 04855.
Branch – WHITE HORSE ST
LEEDS.
NAT. TEL. 321 X

Wilson, Möller & C°

PRODUCE IMPORTERS

& Commission Merchants.

4 S⁺ NICHOLAS BUILDINGS, *Newcastle on Tyne*

W A W.
June 2nd, *190* 8.

William Sample, Esq,

        Bothal,

            Near M O R P E T H.

Dear Sir,

        Mr. William Rutherford, the tenant of Harelaw, Stanton
Estate, which adjoins the Duke of Portland's wood, complains about the
water which flows out of the Duke's wood on to the Harelaw land, and forms
a sort of bog at the bottom. He states that every ewe put out this summer
on this land, has died. The drain near the wicket gate in the Duke's wood
gets silted up with sand and leaves, which diverts the water out of its
natural course, and your men who have been sent to put the matter right,
instead of cleaning it out, have simply turned the water on to the Stanton
Estate. Daniel Leighton informs me that some years ago, Mr. Nathaniel
Clark, who was then agent for the Stanton Estate, laid a complaint before
your Mr. Clark, of Bothal, who promised to have the matter attended to, and
the water carried by its natural channel.
        I should esteem it a great favour if you would have this
matter attended to.

          Yours faithfully,

               William Wilson

Plate 34: Mr Wilson's Letter of Complaint. N.C.A: Ref: ZSA 3-72a.

Gorfenletch Wood Species List 2002-2016

Botanical Name	Common Name	Qty	Year(s) Planted
Acer platanoides	Norway maple	50	2014
Acer pseudoplatanus	Sycamore	325	2012-2013
Aesculus hippocastanum	Horse chestnut	1	2011
Alnus glutinosa	Common alder	1675	2005-2010
Betula pendula	Silver birch	650	2003-2008
Betula pubescens	Downy birch	25	2014
Castanea sativa	Sweet chestnut	8	2004
Corylus avellana	Hazel	500	2003-2009
Crataegus monogyna	Hawthorn	725	2002-2010
Euonymous europaeus	Spindle	75	2005
Fraxinus excelsior	Ash	900	2003-2012
Ilex aquifolium	Holly	205	2003-2008
Iris pseudacorus	Flag lily (pond)	66	2012-2014
Lonicera periclymenum	Honeysuckle	8	2005
Malus sylvestris	Crab apple	100	2002-2008
Picea sitchensis	Sitka spruce	1800	2013-2015
Pinus sylvestris	Scots pine	1100	2003-2005
Populus nigra	Black poplar	294	2011-2012
Populus tremula	Aspen	400	2012-2015
Prunus avium	Wild cherry	400	2003-2016
Prunus padus	Bird cherry	250	2003
Prunus spinosa	Black thorn	350	2003
Quercus petraea	Sessile oak	450	2003-2009
Quercus robur	English oak	1195	2014-2016
Quercus rubra	Red oak	25	2013
Rosa arvensis & canina	Field & dog rose	675	2002-2006

Salix alba caerulea	Crick' bat willow	100	2003-2014
Salix caprea	Goat willow	75	2004-2007
Salix fragilis	Crack willow	250	2009
Salix viminalis	Osier willow	500	2003-2006
Salix wallingtonia	Grey willow	1	2011
Sambucus nigra	Elder	1	2009
Sorbus aucuparia	Rowan	326	2003-2014
Tilia cordata	Small leaf lime	230	2004-2016
Typha latifolia	Reed (pond)	60	2014
Ulex europaeus	Gorse	875	2002-2010
Ulmus glabra	Wych elm	75	2003-2006
Viburnum opulus	Guelder rose	150	2002-2005

Acknowledgements

To Charles, Ed and Janice of Trees Please Ltd who supplied the saplings, stakes, shelters and requisites for the Wood.

Bill and Rachel of Air images Ltd for the aerial surveys, view of the original field and the use of the photographs.

Simon and Tracy for their expertise on plants, pond excavation and who together with Peter and Ann, John and Maggie donated trees to the Wood.

Andy and Ann for pond plans and assistance with the owl box.

The Woodland neighbours, John and Ann, Peter, Joanna and family, Graham.

Head Gardener John and his staff at Wallington Hall, Northumberland.

Northumberland County Archives for Mr Wilson's letter, maps and research guidance.

My enthusiastic and encouraging editor Debz Hobbs-Wyatt.

Elizabeth for her patience with my early morning starts and grubby home comings.

To everyone who gave their time and enthusiasm for the Woodland project. It would be impossible to name all without the danger of omitting one or two.

Many thanks, there is a tree in the Wood for each of you.

* * * *

Lightning Source UK Ltd.
Milton Keynes UK
UKHW05f0342260518
323218UK00007B/137/P